Planetarium

To Mary
C. W.

To Kamini, Vikas, and Sachin
R. P.

Estimates of planetary size and distance can vary depending on the method
of measurement, among other factors. The numbers herein reflect current data,
but new discoveries are being made all the time.

First U.S. edition 2019
First published by Big Picture Press (U.K.) 2018

Library of Congress Catalog Card Number 2018961329.
ISBN 978-1-5362-0623-4

19 20 21 22 23 24 WKT 10 9 8 7 6 5 4 3

Printed in Shenzhen, Guangdong, China

This book was typeset in Gill Sans and Mrs. Green.
The illustrations are digital engravings.

BIG PICTURE PRESS
an imprint of
Candlewick Press
99 Dover Street
Somerville, Massachusetts 02144

www.candlewick.com

This book was produced in association with the Science Museum, London.
Science Museum logo © SCMG Enterprises Ltd.
www.sciencemuseum.org.uk

Welcome
to the
Museum

ADMIT ALL

Planetarium

illustrated by CHRIS WORMELL

written by RAMAN PRINJA

BPP

Preface

Starting just 62 miles/100 kilometers above our planet, space is an airless, soundless vacuum, stretching farther than we can possibly imagine. It has fascinated humans since our earliest days, but we are only just beginning to unravel its mysteries.

As we peer beyond the horizon of our blue-and-green planet, we cannot help but wonder what lies out there. Over thousands of years, civilizations have begun to piece together a picture of the stars and planets around us, and in the past century we have made extraordinary steps forward in space exploration. We have sent space probes to study every planet in our solar system, we have discovered that the universe started with a big bang, and we have even put humans on the moon. With every passing decade, our knowledge has continued to increase, fueled by constant technological improvements and our unquenchable curiosity.

We are currently at an incredibly exciting time in our exploration of the universe. Over the next decade, the launch of new space probes and the construction of gigantic telescopes will allow us to see farther from our planet than ever before. New observations may offer up clues to some of the universe's great unanswered questions. Are we alone in the universe? Are there universes beyond our own? What does the inside of a black hole look like? There's no knowing what the astronomers of the future could uncover, but beyond a doubt, they will push forward the frontiers of our knowledge.

A great voyage of discovery lies ahead of us—and that voyage begins here in this museum. Enter its pages to step beyond the surface of our planet and begin an interstellar journey like no other.

Professor Raman Prinja
University College, London, England

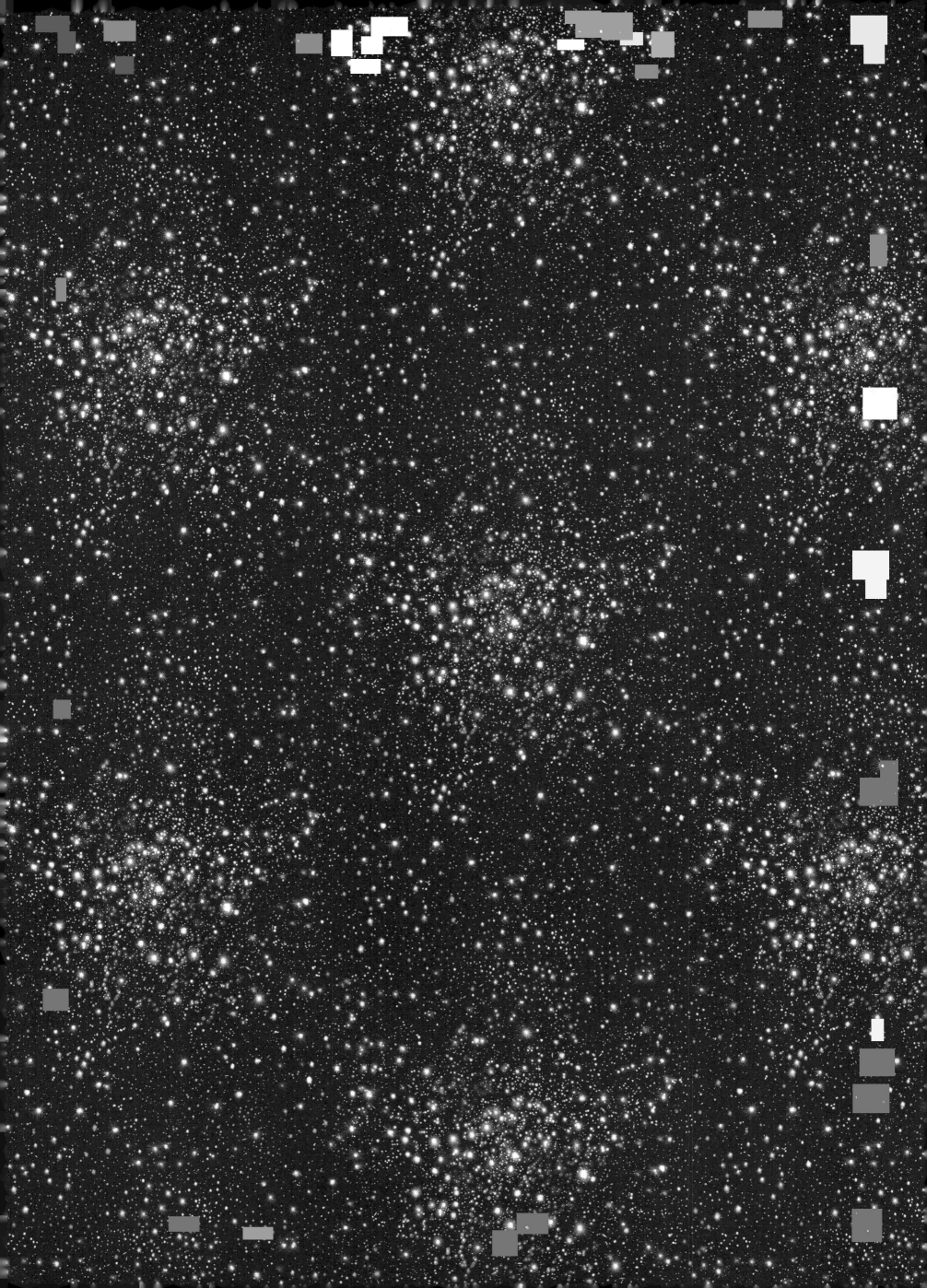

Entrance

Welcome to Planetarium: 1;
Our Place in the Universe: 5

Gallery 1
Looking at Space

Radiation and Light: 8;
Telescopes: 10; Modern Observatories: 12;
Space Telescopes: 14

Gallery 2
The Solar System

The Solar System: 18; Mercury: 20; Venus: 22;
Earth: 24; The Moon: 26; Mars: 28; Jupiter: 30; Saturn: 32;
Uranus: 34; Neptune: 36; Dwarf Planets: 38;
Comets and Asteroids: 40; Exoplanets: 42

Gallery 3
The Sun

The Sun: 46; The Sun-Earth Connection: 48;
The Death of the Sun: 50

Gallery 4
The Night Sky

The Night Sky: 54; Northern Hemisphere Constellations: 56;
Southern Hemisphere Constellations: 58

Gallery 5
The Stars

Star Types: 62; Stellar Births: 64;
The Life Cycle of Stars: 66;
Stellar Deaths: 68;
Black Holes: 70

Gallery 6
Galaxies

Galaxy Types: 74;
The Milky Way Galaxy: 76;
Cosmic Collisions: 78;
Galaxy Clusters: 80

Gallery 7
The Universe

The Universe: 84; The Big Bang: 86;
The Runaway Universe: 88;
The End of the Universe: 90

Library

Index: 94; Curators: 96;
To Learn More: 96

Entrance

Welcome to Planetarium

This book will take you on an intergalactic journey far beyond Earth's boundaries, transporting you across the solar system, through the Milky Way, and on toward the most distant galaxies. Within its galleries you will visit places where no human has ever set foot and view exhibits too large to hold within any museum — except this one.

Take a stroll through the pages of *Planetarium* and watch the universe unfold before you. As you walk the galleries, each chapter will take you farther and farther from Earth before you finally exit through the shop at the end of the universe. Look carefully at the exhibits along your way: they have been carefully collected from across space and time and would take many lifetimes to reach from our planet.

Your tour will begin in the only historic gallery in our collection, which tells the story of astronomy and our ancient fascination with the stars. Here, you will observe many exhibits that can also be seen within the halls of great museums around the world. But as you move on, weaving between planets and asteroids, you will encounter objects too large and strange to be housed in any building. You will see the dusty birth of stars, watch their explosive endings, and come dangerously close to the center of a black hole.

As you approach the final galleries of the museum, prepare to open your mind and stretch your imagination, for here you will encounter the largest structures in existence. Larger than a star, larger than a galaxy, these superclusters stretch across space like a giant spiderweb and can help us understand how the universe began.

This is the only museum to hold whole stars, vast galaxies, and mysterious dark matter within its collections. So enter *Planetarium* here to begin your voyage of discovery, and uncover the many and marvelous wonders of the universe.

Laniakea Supercluster

Universe

Solar System

Earth

Our Place in the Universe

The universe is unimaginably vast and contains absolutely everything, from the tiniest atoms to giant galaxies. Despite this incredible amount of matter, the universe is still so immense that most of it is completely empty.

Contemplating the scale of the universe is a daunting task. One starting point is to think about Earth's place within it by imagining our "cosmic address." So, rather than writing down a house number, street, town, and country, we replace each line with larger and larger structures in space.

Our cosmic address starts with our planet, Earth, which is one of several planets within the solar system. The star at the heart of the solar system, the sun, is one of around two hundred billion stars in the Milky Way galaxy, and in turn, our galaxy is one of about fifty in a cluster called the Local Group. This combines with other galaxy clusters to form the Virgo Supercluster, and finally the Virgo Supercluster is just part of a vast region in space called the Laniakea Supercluster, which contains around a hundred million billion stars. This means that our cosmic address is: Earth, solar system, Milky Way galaxy, Local Group, Virgo Supercluster, Laniakea Supercluster.

Even if we understand where we fit within the universe, understanding its scale is another matter. For such vast distances, everyday units of measurement such as kilometers or miles are not useful. Instead, astronomers use a unit called a light-year: this is the distance that light can travel in one year. Since light has a speed of 200,000 miles/300,000 kilometers per second, the distance it travels in a single year is 5.9 trillion miles/9.5 trillion kilometers. Traveling at this speed, you could fly around Earth seven and a half times in one second!

Now imagine traveling from your house to the next street, or even the next town—but doing this with your cosmic address. The distance between our sun and the planet Neptune is 0.0005 light-years. The Milky Way is 100,000 light-years across. But largest of all, the universe—with its estimated ten trillion galaxies—is an astounding 93 billion light-years wide.

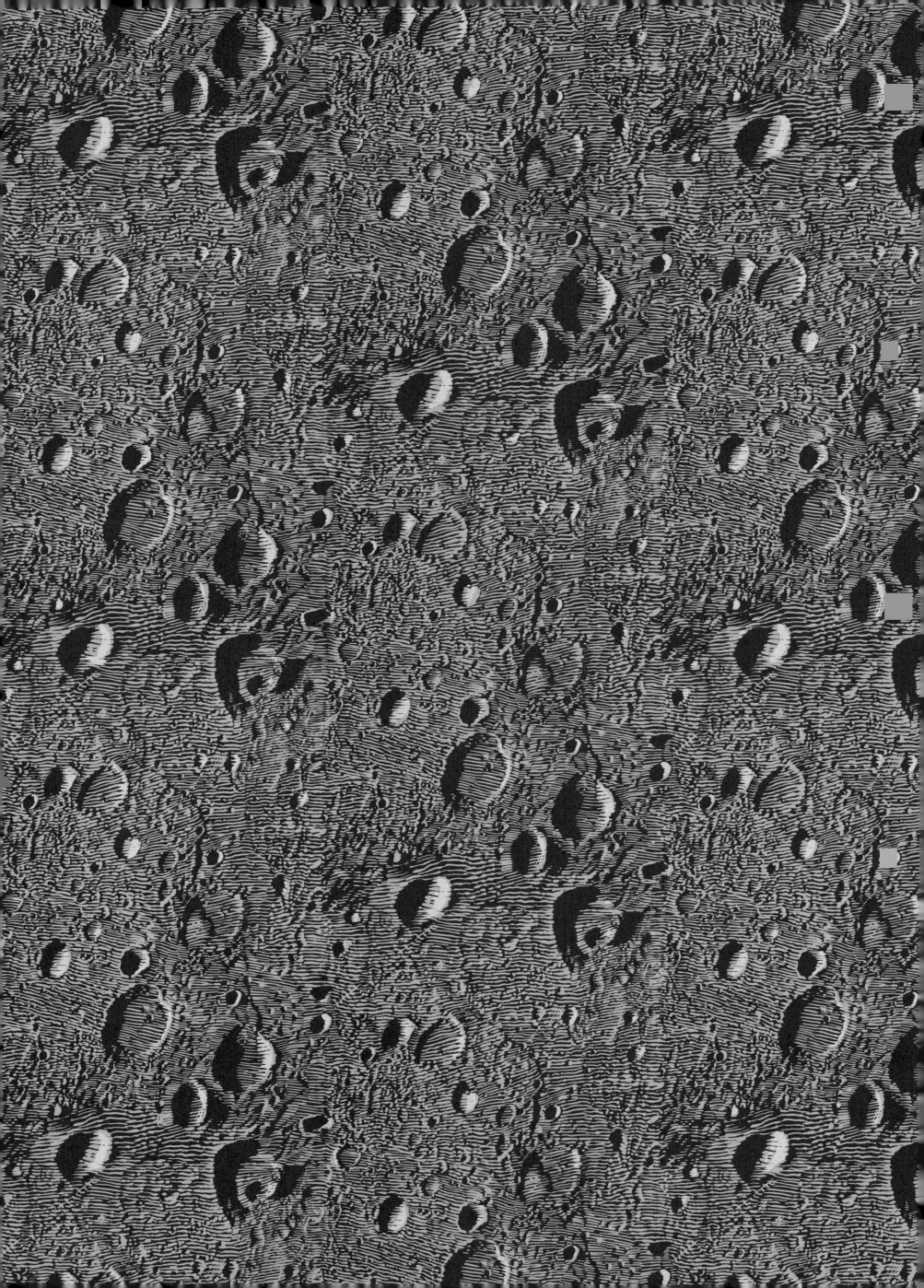

Gallery 1

Looking at Space

Radiation and Light
Telescopes
Modern Observatories
Space Telescopes

Radiation and Light

Stars and galaxies are so far away that we have no chance of visiting them. Everything we know about these distant objects comes from studying the energy, or radiation, they emit.

Light is the only radiation we can see with our eyes, but there are other types we cannot see, including gamma rays, X-rays, ultraviolet radiation, infrared radiation, microwaves, and radio waves. They travel through space as waves of varying lengths, collectively known as the electromagnetic spectrum. This spectrum is often drawn as a line with the shortest wavelengths (the distance between each crest of the waves) at one end and the longest at the other. The sizes of wavelengths range from a fraction of an atom (in the case of gamma rays) to larger than a building (for radio waves).

Each type of wave is emitted by different objects and events in space, so they can be studied by astronomers to tell us more about the universe. For example, gamma rays are seen emerging from the most violent explosions in the universe (like when two stars collide); X-rays can be emitted by exploding stars; and infrared light is given off by some of the coldest objects in space, such as the dusty clouds in which new stars are born.

Even the light we see, known as "visible light," is made up of different parts. We see these components when water droplets in the air split sunlight to form a rainbow across the sky. The red, orange, yellow, green, blue, indigo, and violet colors of a rainbow can also be seen by passing white light through a glass prism. Astronomers use this technique to split visible light from stars into its component parts so they can study the chemical makeup, speed, and temperatures of these burning balls of gas.

--------------------- *Key to plate* ---------------------

1: **The electromagnetic spectrum**

a) Gamma rays
b) X-rays
c) Ultraviolet radiation
d) Visible light
e) Infrared radiation
f) Microwaves
g) Radio waves

Different radiation types are classified by their wavelengths (the distance between the crests of each wave) and their frequencies (the number of waves in a space of time). Gamma rays have the highest frequencies and shortest wavelengths, while radio waves have the lowest frequencies and longest wavelengths.

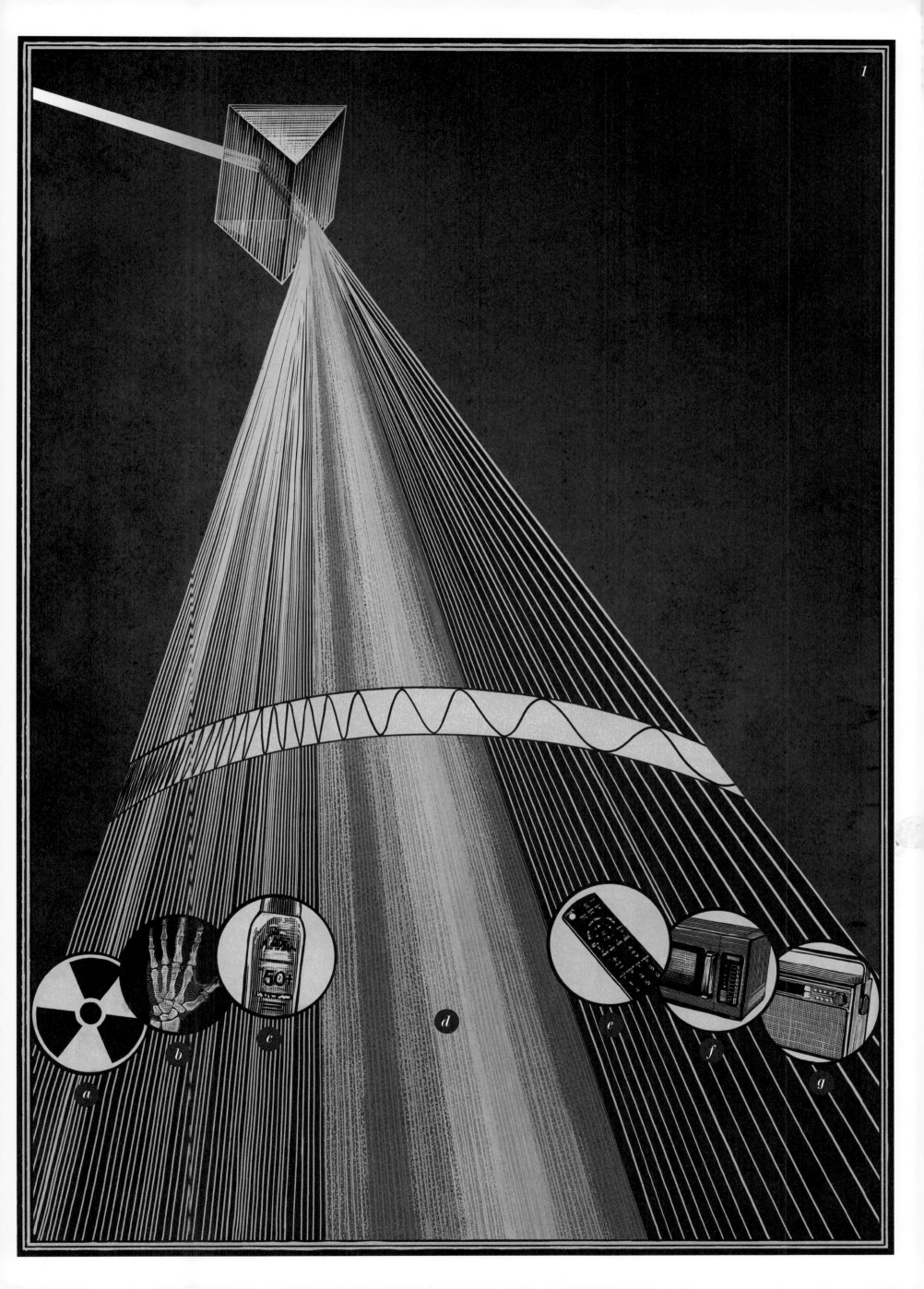

Telescopes

When we gaze at the night sky, we see thousands of stars as tiny pinpricks of light. Even with the naked eye, we can track their position as Earth rotates and note their varying colors and brightnesses. However, in order to truly study them, we depend on telescopes—optical instruments that make distant objects appear much larger.

Objects in space, such as stars and galaxies, are very far away, and only a tiny amount of the light they create reaches Earth. This is because the particles in light spread out as they move farther from their source, making their light appear dimmer. Telescopes function like buckets for collecting this faint light. Just as a bigger bucket catches more rainwater, a bigger telescope gathers more light, and this makes fainter images much brighter. Whereas the pupils of our eyes are barely 1/5 inch/5 millimeters in diameter, modern telescopes can be more than 33 feet/10 meters wide. A telescope this size can see objects four million times fainter than those seen with the unaided eye.

Telescopes work in three steps: first, they collect light using a lens or mirror; then the light is focused into a small, sharp image; finally, this image is magnified. Before the nineteenth century, astronomers simply looked at the magnified image with their eyes and made wonderful drawings of what they saw. Today, the images made by large telescopes are recorded electronically, then stored on computers for analysis. The light can also be passed through a spectroscope to learn more about the wavelengths emitted by the object.

The two main types of telescope are refractors and reflectors. Refracting telescopes use lenses to bend, or refract, light. The light enters through the front lens and travels through the telescope to the eyepiece, where it is magnified. Reflecting telescopes use mirrors to reflect light. Light enters the telescope, bounces off a curved primary mirror, then is reflected off a smaller, secondary mirror, which magnifies the image.

Key to plate

1: **Galileo's x20 telescope**

Lens width: 1 1/2 inches/37 millimeters
This imagined view shows famous astronomer Galileo Galilei using a refracting telescope in 1609. It was one of the first telescopes ever made. Galileo's observations revealed mountains and craters on the moon and, in 1610, revealed Jupiter's four largest moons.

2: **Herschel's 40-foot reflecting telescope**

Mirror width: 47 inches/
120 centimeters
William Herschel started constructing the telescope in 1785 and began observations with it in 1789. At the time, it was the largest telescope in the world. Herschel used it to study the moons of Saturn.

3: **James Lick telescope**

Lens width: 36 inches/91 centimeters
At the time of its construction in 1888, this was the largest refracting telescope in the world—it is the third largest today. Its dome can rotate, and its floor can be raised and lowered to bring the viewer closer to the telescope. James Lick is buried under the floor at the base of the telescope.

Modern Observatories

We've come a long way since astronomers used the first telescopes in the seventeenth century to look at the moon and our nearest planets. Since then, incredible technological developments have enabled us to see even farther into space, looking far beyond our solar system and even our galaxy. Over the past century, telescope technology has taken a huge step forward thanks to increasingly sophisticated cameras, detectors, spectroscopes, and computers, and to the sheer size of modern telescopes. The power of a telescope is mainly determined by its size, and the mirrors in some can be 33 feet/ 10 meters wide. (Refracting lenses become too heavy at these large sizes so are not used in modern telescopes.) Huge research telescopes, used mainly to study visible light, are housed in multistory buildings called observatories, which are usually perched high on mountaintops, where the air is clear, calm, and dry. Together with dark night skies, these conditions help greatly in obtaining the sharpest possible images.

The next generation of ground-based telescopes will be larger than anything that predates them and will allow us to see objects in space that have never been seen before. One example is the European Extremely Large Telescope (ELT). Once assembled, it will have a diameter of 128 feet/39 meters and be able to detect visible and infrared light, gathering eight million times more light than the telescope used by Galileo in 1609. It will detect light that has taken millions or even billions of years to reach Earth, so the astronomers who use it will essentially be looking back in time to a younger universe! Their studies will answer questions about the origins of planets, stars, galaxies, and the universe.

Key to plate

1: Atacama Large Millimeter Array (ALMA)

Located in the Atacama Desert in Chile, each of ALMA's sixty-six antennae detect radio waves, including low-energy emissions from new stars and young galaxies. The detectors are kept at −501°F/−269°C to avoid background heat blurring their signals.

2: Keck Observatory

Its twin telescopes are 13,800 feet/ 4,200 meters high on Mauna Kea, Hawaii. Each primary mirror is 33 feet/ 10 meters wide and made of thirty-six hexagonal pieces. Computers move the segments so they act as a single reflecting glass. They can detect light as faint as a candle on Earth's moon!

3: Very Large Telescope (VLT)

Placed high on a mountain in the Atacama Desert in Chile, the VLT enjoys some of the clearest night skies on Earth. Each of its four telescopes has a primary mirror 27 feet/8.2 meters wide. Signals from up to three of the telescopes can be combined to increase their power.

Space Telescopes

Earth is surrounded by a blanket of gases called the atmosphere, which contains the air we breathe and shields our planet against harmful rays from the sun. Fortunately, we can see right through the atmosphere to the planets and stars beyond it, but when we come to study these objects in detail, the atmosphere can present some problems: moving pockets of air obscure images taken by visible-light telescopes, and the atmosphere can block out whole parts of the electromagnetic spectrum. To obtain the clearest images of space and detect the whole of the electromagnetic spectrum, astronomers have to position their telescopes high above the atmosphere.

Astronomers began to get around this problem in the 1950s by attaching telescopes to large helium-filled balloons that carried their instruments up above the lower layers of air. However, it soon became clear that what they really needed were free-flying telescopes in orbit around Earth. During the late 1960s, several astronomical satellites were successfully launched, mounted with the first gamma ray, X-ray, and ultraviolet telescopes to be placed in orbit. Then, between April 1990 and August 2003, NASA launched its four "Great Observatories" into space, marking a whole new era in space exploration. Each telescope was designed to examine a particular part of the electromagnetic spectrum. The Compton Gamma Ray Observatory (which returned to Earth in 2000) observed gamma rays; the Chandra X-ray Observatory observes X-rays; the Spitzer Space Telescope observes infrared light; and the Hubble Space Telescope observes visible and near-ultraviolet light (after a service mission in 1997, it can also detect near-infrared light). The Hubble has sent back some of the most stunning images of space ever taken.

At the forefront of the next era of space telescopes will be the James Webb Space Telescope (JWST), orbiting at a vantage point 900,000 miles/1.5 million kilometers away from Earth. It will use infrared vision to peer more than 13.5 billion light-years away into the darkness of the earliest times of the universe.

--- *Key to plate* ---

1: James Webb Space Telescope
Location: 900,000 miles/1.5 million kilometers above Earth
Launch: Scheduled 2020
This space telescope will study every main phase in the history of the universe. It will also be six times more powerful than the Hubble telescope.

2: Spitzer Space Telescope
Location: 140 million miles/230 million kilometers above Earth
Launched: August 25, 2003
This infrared telescope has a liquid helium tank that keeps its instruments at −458°F/−272°C, close to absolute zero, the lowest temperature possible.

3: Hubble Space Telescope
Location: 342 miles/550 kilometers above Earth
Launched: April 24, 1990
Hubble's main telescope collects about 40,000 times more light than the human eye.

4: Fermi Gamma-ray Space Telescope
Location: 342 miles/550 kilometers above Earth
Launched: June 11, 2008
This gamma-ray telescope detects the most high-energy objects in the universe. Gamma rays are given off by mysterious objects such as black holes and exploding stars.

5: Chandra X-ray Observatory
Location: max. 86,000 miles/139,000 kilometers above Earth
Launched: July 23, 1999
Chandra detects X-rays emitted by very hot objects such as exploded stars and galaxy clusters.

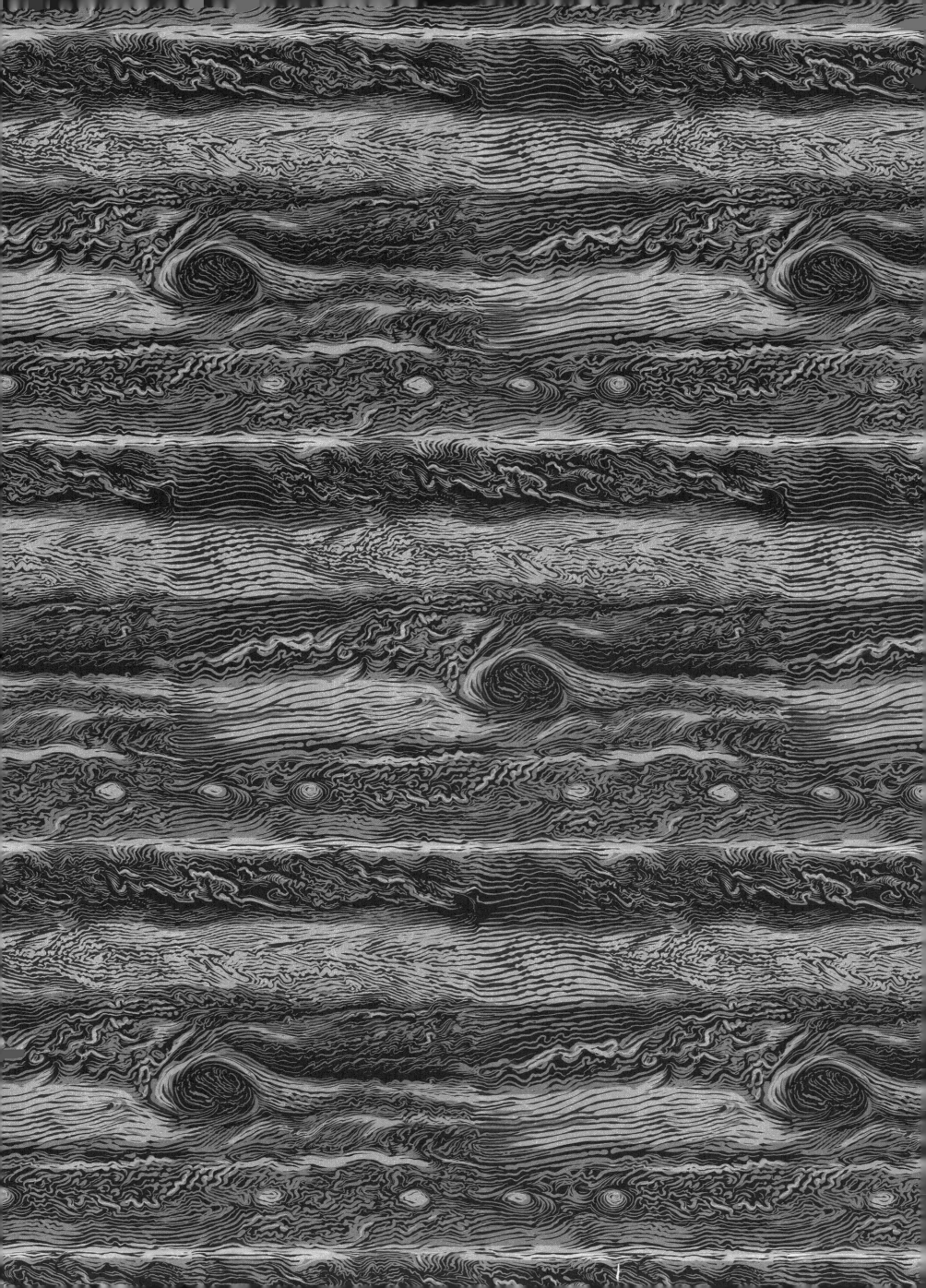

The Solar System

The Solar System

Mercury

Venus

Earth

The Moon

Mars

Jupiter

Saturn

Uranus

Neptune

Dwarf Planets

Comets and Asteroids

Exoplanets

The Solar System

The solar system is a collection of eight planets, more than 180 moons, and millions of smaller objects, all orbiting a star called the sun. Staggeringly, the sun contains more than 99 percent of all the mass in the solar system, and its enormous size means it has a very powerful gravitational force. This exerts a pull on the planets around it, just as gravity on Earth pulls you to the ground and makes things fall. However, the planets will never fall into the sun because the sideways movement of their orbits balances the sun's gravitational pull—like a ball swinging on a piece of string around a central point. In this way, the sun's gravity holds the solar system together, keeping everything—from the biggest planets to the smallest rocks—in flat, ordered orbits.

The largest objects in the solar system after the sun are the planets. The innermost four—Mercury, Venus, Earth, and Mars—are terrestrial planets, with solid, rocky surfaces. Beyond Mars, across a belt of millions of asteroids, lie the four gas planets: Jupiter, Saturn, Uranus, and Neptune. They are gigantic, with masses from fifteen to three hundred times that of Earth, and have no solid surface, as they are surrounded by cloud layer after layer.

The solar system started to form about 4.6 billion years ago, forged out of a cloud of gas and dust that collapsed under the force of its own gravity. Over hundreds of millions of years, the collapse speeded up the rotation of the gas and dust and spread it out into a flat disc—in the same way a baker spins dough in the air to make a flat pizza. Slowly, a huge amount of compressed matter gathered in the center of the disc and made the sun. The rest of the material from the cloud then clumped together to form the planets and their moons.

From our earliest days, humans have been fascinated by the solar system. Spacecraft have documented every planet within it and borne witness to amazing sights, from ice volcanoes on the dwarf planet Pluto to diamond hailstones on Neptune. But despite all that we have learned, we still have many more discoveries to make about the incredible system we call home.

Key to plate

1: **The sun**

2: **Mercury**
Distance from the sun: 0.4 AU
(An AU—Astronomical Unit—is
the distance from Earth to the sun.)
Orbital period: 88 Earth days

3: **Venus**
Distance from the sun: 0.7 AU
Orbital period: 224.7 Earth days

4: **Earth**
Distance from the sun: 1.0 AU
Orbital period: 365.2 Earth days

5: **Mars**
Distance from the sun: 1.5 AU
Orbital period: 1.8 Earth years

6: **Jupiter**
Distance from the sun: 5.2 AU
Orbital period: 11.9 Earth years

7: **Saturn**
Distance from the sun: 9.6 AU
Orbital period: 29.4 Earth years

8: **Uranus**
Distance from the sun: 19.2 AU
Orbital period: 84.1 Earth years

9: **Neptune**
Distance from the sun: 30.1 AU
Orbital period: 164.8 Earth years

Mercury

Mercury is a hot, rocky planet just a third the size of Earth. It is the smallest and fastest planet in the solar system—zooming through space at 105,900 miles per hour/ 170,500 kilometers per hour—and is also the closest planet to the sun. If you could stand on Mercury's surface, the nearby sun would appear three times larger in the sky than it looks to us on Earth. This proximity to the sun means Mercury is very difficult to see from Earth except at twilight. However, about thirteen times a century, observers can see Mercury pass the face of the sun as a small dark dot.

Like Earth, Mercury is a terrestrial rocky planet, with a solid iron-nickel core and a surface surprisingly similar to that of our moon. Its smooth plains are thought to have been made by ancient lava flows, while its numerous craters were most likely carved out by meteoroid and comet impacts. Above its surface it has a very thin, temporary atmosphere. This is continually created as the solar wind (a stream of charged gas released by the sun) streams past the planet, leaving behind traces of hydrogen and helium gas, but also knocking atoms off the planet's surface. This creates a fine layer of gas that rises and escapes into space almost as soon as it is made. Without a substantial atmosphere to trap the planet's heat, and with the sun's searing surface so near, Mercury experiences extreme heat and cold as the planet rotates. Temperatures soar to 644°F/340°C during the day, then plummet to an air-freezing −292°F/−180°C at night: the most extreme range of temperatures experienced anywhere in the solar system.

The MESSENGER probe (operational 2011–2015) discovered that, despite these fierce daytime temperatures, there are pockets of water ice at Mercury's north pole, where the planet has deep craters permanently shielded from the sun's heat. Scientists believe that this water was most likely delivered to Mercury by icy comets smashing into the planet during the early history of the solar system.

Key to plate

1: **Mercury**
Diameter: 3,032 miles/
4,879 kilometers
Orbital period (year): 88 Earth days
Rotation period (day): 1,407.6 hours
Known moons: None
Owing to its fast orbit, Mercury was named after the fleet-footed Roman messenger god. It was first recorded by an Assyrian astronomer

in the fourteenth century BCE. Mercury's wide, flat plains were formed by ancient volcanic activity and are interspersed with craters and long, rugged cliffs.

2: **Cross-section of the interior**
a) Core
b) Mantle
c) Crust

Mercury has a dense iron-nickel core at least three-quarters the size of its overall radius. The latest data from the MESSENGER mission shows that the planet has a weak magnetic field, suggesting that its core is at least partly molten. Above the core is a 300-mile-/500-kilometer-thick layer called the mantle, then an even thinner surface crust.

THE SOLAR
SYSTEM

Venus

Venus and Earth are often referred to as sister planets due to their similar size, density, and internal structure, but that is where their similarities end. Unlike Earth, Venus is a hostile, cloud-covered world with an atmosphere so thick that its surface pressure is about ninety times that on Earth. Not only would this pressure crush anyone who stood on the planet's surface, but its carbon-dioxide atmosphere would be poisonous to breathe, and the intense heat would boil them. Venus is the hottest planet in the solar system.

From Earth, Venus appears as the second-brightest body in the sky at night (after our moon). But looking at it through a telescope, we can see nothing of the planet's surface beneath its thick, unbroken cloud cover. Space probes reveal that this dense atmosphere is almost 50 miles/80 kilometers thick, and 97 percent of it consists of poisonous carbon dioxide. The thick blanket of gas acts like a greenhouse, trapping heat from the sun so that it builds up, creating temperatures of up to 864°F/462°C—hot enough to melt tin and lead. This toxic atmosphere is also the site of vast, dramatic thunderstorms, which rain down sulfuric acid and can make around twenty lightning flashes a second.

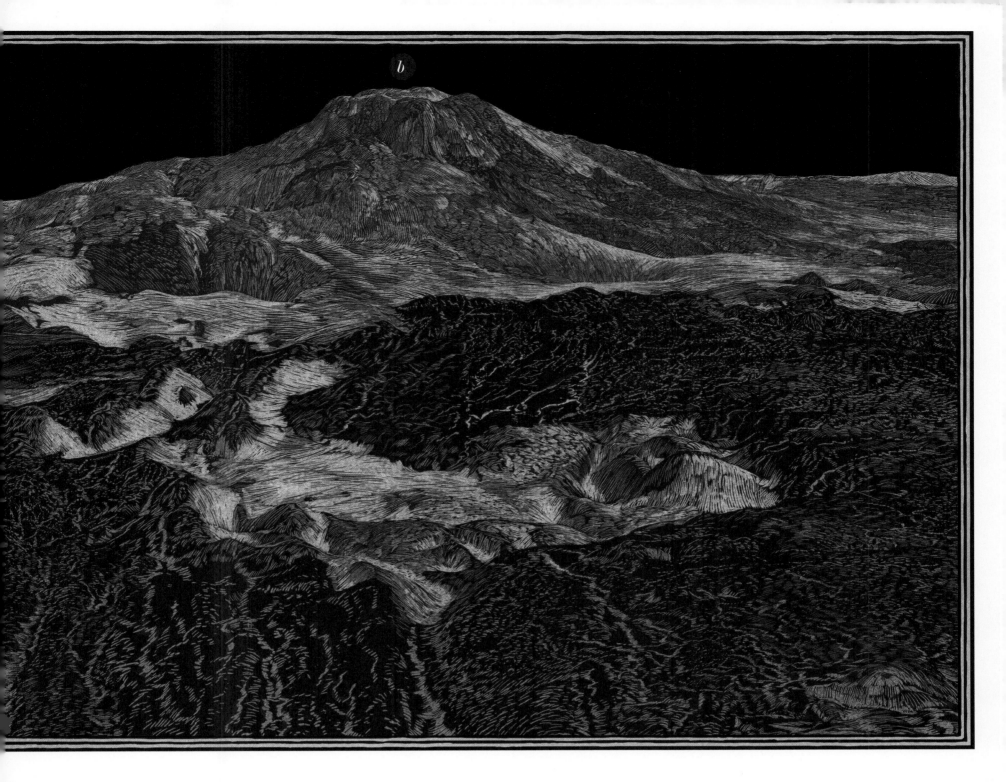

b

In order to get a global view of the surface of Venus, astronomers rely on space probes: the Magellan and Venus Express spacecraft have both been sent to orbit the planet. They bounce radar off the planet's surface to build three-dimensional maps and images of its terrain. The data collected has revealed a spectacular range of surface features, including dormant volcanoes, sand dunes, ancient lava plains, and rough highland regions. The absence of ancient craters also suggests that lava from extensive volcanic activity completely resurfaced the planet between three hundred million and five hundred million years ago.

Key to plate

1: **Venus**

Diameter: 7,521 miles/
12,104 kilometers
Orbital period (year): 224.7 Earth days
Rotation period (day): 5,832.5 hours
Known moons: None
Venus was named after the Roman goddess of love and beauty. Its first known observation was made by Babylonian astronomers in the seventeenth century BCE.

a) **Planet surface**

Large extinct volcanic mountains can be seen on Venus's surface. Shield volcanoes formed billions of years ago when hot, fluid lava bubbled up above the ground. The volcanoes can be a few miles/kilometers tall and hundreds of miles/kilometers wide. Venus has more than 1,600 major extinct volcanoes, which is more than any other planet in the solar system.

b) **Maat Mons**

Named after the Egyptian goddess of justice, Maat Mons is Venus's second-highest volcano. It has an elevation of 5 miles/8 kilometers and a diameter of 245 miles/395 kilometers. The mountain is covered in ancient lava, giving it a smooth, sloping surface that reflects brightly in radar images. Astronomers believe that the lava may have flowed as recently as ten million years ago.

Earth

Our home planet, Earth, is the only body in the solar system known to support life. Since its formation 4.56 billion years ago, it has transformed from a violent, molten rock into a world of deep oceans, lush forests, and sandy deserts, supporting an incredible range of life-forms. It is a unique planet in the solar system for the vast volumes of liquid water that cover two-thirds of its surface and for its thin, oxygen-rich atmosphere.

Earth's atmosphere not only contains the oxygen we breathe but also acts as a shield, protecting us from the sun's radiation and burning up space debris such as meteors as they approach. From the ground up, the atmosphere has five main layers: the troposphere (where water vapor is found and where all weather takes place), the stratosphere (which contains the ozone), the mesosphere (where meteors burn up), the thermosphere (where the International Space Station orbits), and the exosphere (which is very thin and merges into outer space).

Beneath Earth's surface, its interior is split into distinct layers, which we can detect by studying the movement of shock waves after an earthquake. At its center is the core, a dense, solid ball of nickel-iron as hot as the surface of the sun. Above this is the outer core, where whirlpools of molten iron generate Earth's magnetic field (an invisible force field stretching around the planet). Above the core is Earth's thickest layer, the mantle, formed of solid rock so hot that it starts to flow like a liquid. And last of all is the hard crust, a fine outer layer surrounding the planet. This is so thin compared with the other layers that it is like a postage stamp on the outside of a beach ball. The crust and part of the mantle together form huge slabs called tectonic plates. These shift over the molten part of the mantle, moving a few centimeters a year (about the same rate that fingernails grow). Most geologic activity, including volcanic eruptions, violent earthquakes, and mountain formation, occurs as a result of the plates slowly shifting.

Key to plate

1: **Earth**

Diameter: 7,926 miles/
12,756 kilometers
Orbital period (year): 365.2 Earth days
Rotation period (day): 23.9 hours
Known moons: One

Viewed from space, Earth is often described as a "blue marble," owing to the reflection of blue-sky light off its watery surface. Almost 71 percent of its surface is covered with water; 3.5 percent of this is fresh water

contained in lakes, glaciers, and ice, but the rest is found in the saltwater oceans. Astronomers believe most of it was brought to Earth billions of years ago by icy comets and meteoroids from the outer solar system.

The Moon

The moon formed at the same time as Earth, when a body of rock about the size of Mars crashed into our planet. The debris that was flung out from the impact slowly collected under gravity to form a moon, kept in orbit around Earth by our planet's stronger gravitational force. As a result of this formation, Earth and the moon share many of the same materials. No other satellite is so close in composition or size to its parent planet. To understand their relative sizes, imagine Earth as a basketball and the moon as a tennis ball 24 feet/7.4 meters away. (Using this comparison, the sun would be the size of a large house almost 2 miles/3 kilometers away!)

The moon takes the same time to spin on its axis as it takes to complete a single orbit of the Earth (around twenty-seven days), which means we always see exactly the same side of the moon. This is known as synchronized rotation. When the moon appears to shine, it is in fact reflecting the sun's light. Viewed from Earth, different amounts of its surface are lit up, creating the phases of the moon. The lunar phases appear different in each hemisphere. In the north, the waxing crescent grows from the right. In the south, it grows from the left.

The distant surface of the moon is covered in powdery soil, craters, dead volcanoes, and wide, lava-covered plains. These lunar plains are known as *maria,* which is the Latin word for "seas." From Earth they appear as shadowy areas, whereas the mountainous highlands appear much brighter. Since the moon has no significant atmosphere to block the sun's rays or trap heat at night, its temperature varies greatly between day and night, with average temperatures of −297°F/−183°C at night and 223°F/106°C during the day.

The moon is the only body in space, other than Earth, where humans have set foot. Only six crewed moon landings have taken place, starting with Neil Armstrong and Buzz Aldrin in July 1969 and ending with Eugene Cernan and Harrison Schmitt in December 1972.

Key to plate

1: **The far side of the moon**
Never seen from Earth, the far side of the moon is riddled with craters. The crust here is thicker than the crust on the Earth-facing side, meaning lava did not emerge so easily here during the moon's period of volcanic activity billions of years ago. The near side has been smoothed out by lava, which filled its craters to form flat *maria,* while the far side is much more densely cratered.

2: **Lunar phases (as seen from the southern hemisphere)**
The moon's appearance changes depending on its orbit and the viewer's location. These changes are known as lunar phases. During the first phase, the new moon, the moon reflects no light so is invisible to us. After this we see:
a) Waxing crescent
b) First quarter
c) Waxing gibbous
d) Full moon

e) Waning gibbous
f) Last quarter
g) Waning crescent
This cycle ends with a return to a new moon and takes an average of 29.5 days to complete.

1

2a *2b* *2c* *2d* *2e* *2f* *2g*

THE SOLAR
SYSTEM

Mars

The last of the four terrestrial planets in our solar system, Mars is known as the "red planet" for its distinctive rusty color, which can be seen with the naked eye. This bloody tinge led the ancient Greeks to name the planet Ares, after their war god, and today we know it as Mars, after the Roman god of war. Ancient Chinese astronomers also knew the planet for its blazing color and called it the "fire star."

The reason for Mars's red hue is that its surface material contains a lot of iron oxide: the same combination of iron and oxygen that gives blood and rust their red color. Most terrestrial planets, such as Earth, have dense iron cores, as gravity quickly pulled this heavy metal downward after the planets' formation. However, Mars has a smaller mass and weaker gravitational field than the other terrestrial planets, meaning more of its iron remained in its upper layers. This then combined with oxygen to form the reddish fine-grained dust that blankets the planet today.

Alongside its stretching sand dunes, Mars boasts spectacular surface features—from pockmarked craters to gaping valleys—formed over billions of years by volcanic eruptions, asteroid impacts, and the planet's strong winds. Its highest point, Olympus Mons, is the tallest mountain in the solar system, an extinct volcano stretching

13 miles/21 kilometers high—around three times the altitude of Earth's tallest peak, Mount Everest. The planet also has the largest storms in the solar system—raging dust storms that stretch for thousands of miles. During some seasons, they are so severe that they can cover the entire planet.

Although Mars today is a dry, dusty planet, liquid water once flowed over its surface, as evidenced by channels and valleys that must have been made by moving water. This water has long since evaporated, but there remains the possibility that simple bacterial life may have thrived there in the past. Even today, Mars is thought to have liquid water beneath its surface and has thick ice caps at its poles. Spacecraft are currently exploring the planet and its atmosphere to find out if bacterial life could ever have existed there.

Key to plate

1: Mars
Diameter: 4,220 miles/6,792 kilometers
Orbital period (year): 1.8 Earth years
Rotation period (day): 24.6 hours
Known moons: 2
Mars is named after the Roman god of war. The planet was known about as far back as the sixteenth century BCE, when the Egyptians named it after their falcon-headed god, Horus.

a) Phobos
This moon orbits 3,604 miles/5,800 kilometers above Mars's surface. It is predicted that it could be destroyed by gravitational forces in about seven million years, and that the debris will form a thin ring around Mars.

b) Deimos
Mars's smaller moon has an irregular shape like an asteroid. Its orbit is getting farther away from Mars, so it will eventually be cast off into space.

Jupiter

Jupiter is the largest planet in the solar system, so big that Earth could fit inside it 1,300 times. Owing to its size and composition, it is known as a "gas giant": a planet with a dense, swirling atmosphere but without any solid surface you could stand on. At its inaccessible center is a solid core of ice, rock, and metal, surrounded by liquid hydrogen. But moving farther from the core, the planet's temperature and pressure decreases, and its elements start to act more like gases, giving way to a thick atmosphere of hydrogen and helium. In Jupiter's outermost layer, ammonia and sulfur create a swirling tapestry of red, yellow, and white; the colors are created by variations in temperature and composition. The gases are pushed into bands of dark "belts" and bright "zones" by the planet's fast rotation—spinning on its axis once every ten hours. Within this atmosphere we can also see oval-shaped storms like hurricanes, the largest of which is called the Great Red Spot. This has been raging continuously for more than three hundred years.

Circling Jupiter are at least sixty-seven moons in varying shapes and sizes. The four largest are Ganymede, Callisto, Io, and Europa, known as the "Galilean satellites" after their discovery by Galileo Galilei in 1610. Each moon is an incredible world in itself: Ganymede is the largest moon in the solar system, Callisto is the most cratered object known to us, Io is covered in active volcanoes, and Europa's surface ice could be hiding an ocean twice as large as all of Earth's oceans combined.

To date, nine different spacecraft have collected images and data of Jupiter. They have discovered that Jupiter's magnetic field is almost twenty thousand times more powerful than Earth's and have beamed back intriguing images of a faint set of rings around the planet—completely invisible through telescopes on Earth.

Key to plate

1: **Jupiter**
Diameter: 88,846 miles/
142,984 kilometers
Orbital period (year): 11.9 Earth years
Rotation period (day): 9.9 hours
Known moons: 67
The Romans named Jupiter after the king of their gods, who was also the

god of the sky and thunder. It was first observed by Babylonian astronomers in the eighth century BCE.

a) **Great Red Spot**
This powerful and violent cyclone spins around once every six Earth days. At 10,000 miles/16,000

kilometers long, it is so large it can be seen using telescopes on Earth.

b) **Ganymede**
This huge moon is larger than the planet Mercury. Its surface is covered in areas of dark and light terrain, with bright frost at both of its poles.

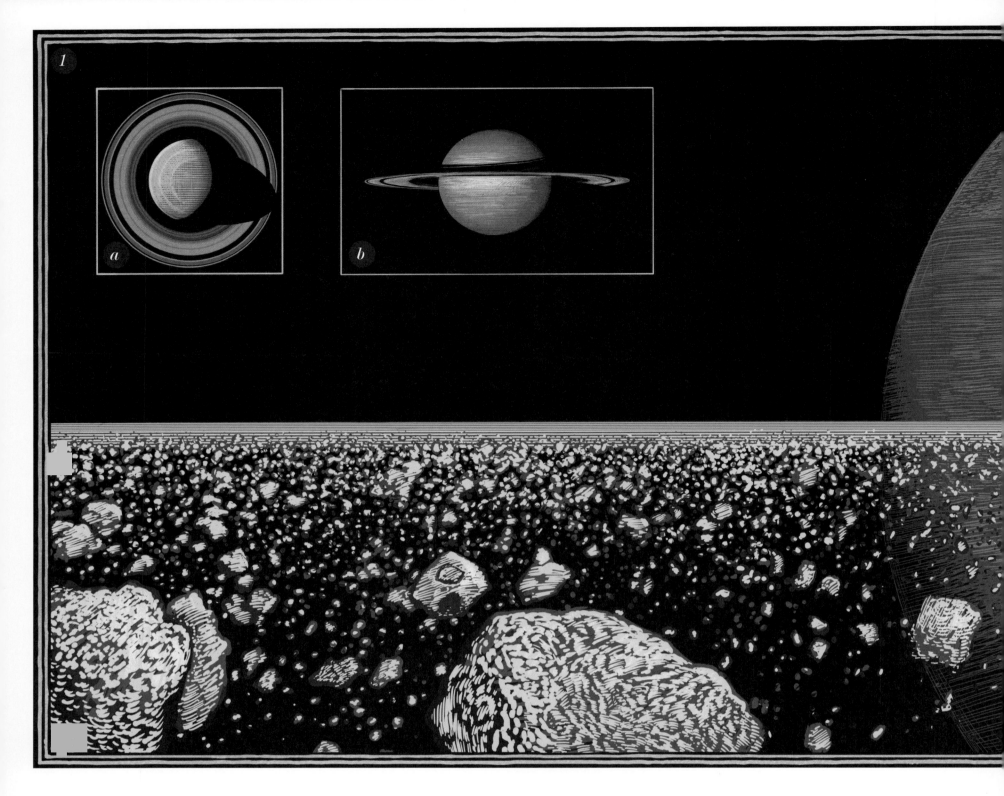

Saturn

Saturn is one of the five planets we can see in the night sky with just our eyes, and it is the most distant planet to have been discovered by ancient civilizations. It is a gas giant surrounded by bright, spectacular rings, for which it is also known as the "ringed planet."

Like Jupiter, Saturn is made mostly of hydrogen and helium, some of the lightest elements in the universe. However, Saturn has just 30 percent of Jupiter's mass and the lowest density of any planet in the solar system. In fact, it would float in water if you could find a bathtub big enough to hold it! Unlike other planets, Saturn radiates almost twice as much heat into space as it receives from the sun. Astronomers think this is generated by droplets of helium falling toward the planet's core and converting from motion into heat energy. This heat powers storms and winds in Saturn's upper atmosphere, with top wind speeds of around 1,100 miles per hour/1,800 kilometers per hour near the equator—faster than even Jupiter's winds. About every thirty years, large storms also break out in this region, seen from above as "Great White Spots" of ammonia crystals.

Encircling Saturn is a system of rings made of billions of ice particles, along with fine dust and house-size boulders. Scientists think the rings formed when a medium-size moon drifted

very close to Saturn and was broken up by the immense force of the planet's gravity. The rings are about 170,000 miles/280,000 kilometers across, but only .6 miles/1 kilometer thick. If you were to build a model of the rings using a meter-wide disk, the disk's thickness would have to be ten thousand times thinner than a razor blade to represent the rings.

Saturn has sixty-two known moons, mostly a mix of rock and water ice. Its moon Titan is the second largest moon in the solar system, with a dense atmosphere of nitrogen. The cold surface of Titan, meanwhile, holds remarkable lakes of liquid methane. This moon is of great interest to scientists searching for extraterrestrial life, as it closely resembles the appearance of Earth at the time when life first evolved on our planet.

─────────────────── *Key to plate* ───────────────────

1: Saturn
Diameter: 74,898 miles/120,536 kilometers
Orbital period (year): 29.4 Earth years
Rotation period (day): 10.7 hours
Known moons: 62
The Romans named Saturn after the father of Jupiter in Roman mythology.

a) **The planet viewed top-down**
During Saturn's orbit, we see its rings from different angles. At times, the rings can be more tipped toward us and seen face-on, as here.

b) **The planet viewed edge-on**
Over many years the rings appear to

close up, showing a narrower aspect, until they appear edge-on and almost invisible. These apparent changes are due to the angle of Saturn's rotational axis relative to the plane (path) of its orbit around the sun.

Uranus

This aqua-blue planet in the outer reaches of the solar system was once considered to be a gas giant like Jupiter and Saturn. However, as astronomers have learned more about its composition and its freezing temperatures, they have reclassified it as an "ice giant." Uranus generates very little heat compared with other planets, so even though it is not as distant from the sun's warmth as its neighbor Neptune, it is still the coldest planet in the solar system. Temperatures within its methane-ice clouds can drop to an incredible −364°F/−220°C. Compositionally, Uranus is also unlike the gas giants, as it has much more methane mixed with the hydrogen and helium in its atmosphere than is found on Jupiter or Saturn. This methane absorbs red light, resulting in the planet's blue-green appearance. We can sometimes glimpse storms in the upper atmosphere scattered across this seemingly smooth surface. These drag up methane ice from the planet's lower layers and can appear as very bright spots when viewed with infrared telescopes.

As it orbits the sun, Uranus adopts an unusual position completely on its side: the axis on which it spins is flipped over by 98°, so its north pole points at the sun for half of its year, and its south pole points at the sun for the remainder of the year. If it were possible for you to stand on the north pole, you would see the sun stay in the sky for forty-two Earth years without ever setting. After this incredibly long "daytime," the sun would finally drop below the horizon, and you would enter forty-two Earth years of "night." Scientists guess that the planet's surprising rotation axis may have resulted from a collision with a large object, which tipped the planet onto its side. The force of this impact could also have created Uranus's thin ring system. Alternatively, the rings could have formed from broken pieces of moon crashing into one another.

Key to plate

1: **Uranus**
Diameter: 31,763 miles/
51,118 kilometers
Orbital period (year): 84.1 Earth years
Rotation period (day): 17.2 hours
Known moons: 27
Uranus was discovered by accident in 1781 by the astronomer William Herschel. Herschel was studying the stars when he noticed an object that appeared to move against them—he realized this must be because the object was closer to us than the stars. At first, Herschel thought he had found a comet. Later, he and other astronomers realized it was a newly discovered planet in orbit around our sun. Although Herschel proposed that the planet should be named Georgium Sidus, after King George III, the planet was named after the Roman god Uranus, who was the father of Saturn.

a) **Bands**
Like other gas planets, Uranus is circled by bands of cloud and haze. These blow around the planet at hundreds of miles per hour.

b) **Rings**
Uranus's outermost ring extends to a radius of 61,000 miles/ 98,000 kilometers from the center of the planet. The rings are relatively young and formed about 600 million years ago out of broken pieces of moons or after a collision between Uranus and a large object.

c) **Miranda**
Miranda is Uranus's smallest moon. Its jumbled-up appearance and broken surface are thought to have resulted from an asteroid impact that made the moon shatter into pieces before it reassembled again under its own gravitational pull.

Neptune

Neptune, the outermost planet in the solar system, gets its beautiful blue color from the methane in its atmosphere. This deep-blue atmosphere is the location of the fastest storms in the solar system. Here, winds race at speeds of up to 1,500 miles per hour/2,400 kilometers per hour—nearly ten times faster than the destructive forces of a Category 5 hurricane on Earth (the most intense winds known on our planet). Neptune also experiences smaller storms that appear as dark spots on its surface, similar to Jupiter's Great Red Spot. These dark spots are shorter-lived than those on Neptune's neighboring planets. Rather than raging for centuries, they can disappear within the space of just a few years. They are often accompanied by clouds of ammonia and water ice, which can be seen as bright white spots in the planet's upper layers. Amazingly, scientists think Neptune's lower atmosphere may also experience "diamond rain," where rising temperature and pressure cause methane to form solid diamonds, which drop down to the planet's center.

Surrounding Neptune are five very faint rings, made of tiny particles that may have been ejected from objects striking the planet's moons. Out of Neptune's fourteen known moons, the most prominent and largest is Triton, which was discovered in October 1846, just seventeen days after Neptune itself was first officially recorded. Triton's surface is mostly made up of rock and ice, with a terrain that mixes craters and smooth plains. Plumes of dust and nitrogen gas erupt out of its crust to give it a very thin atmosphere. And with an average temperature of a chilly −391°F/−235°C, Triton is the coldest known object in the solar system.

Key to plate

1: Neptune

Diameter: 30,775 miles/
49,528 kilometers
Orbital period (year): 164.8 Earth years
Rotation period (day): 16.1 hours
Known moons: 14
Neptune was first observed in 1846 by the German astronomer Johann Gottfried Galle, whose studies were based on the predictions of the French mathematician Urbain Le Verrier. Named after the Roman god of the sea, Neptune is so far out in the solar system that by July 2011 it had only just completed its first full orbit of the sun since its discovery.

a) Great Dark Spot

The Great Dark Spot was an anticyclone (an area of high pressure where the atmosphere is sinking) and was about the same size as Earth. Although this vast storm system was seen by the Voyager 2 probe in 1989, it had disappeared two years later when viewed by Hubble.

2: Cross-section of the interior

a) Core
b) Mantle
c) Atmosphere

The planet has a core of rock and ice that is a little larger than Earth's total mass. It is surrounded by a large mantle (likely a slush of water, ammonia, and methane ices) and then an atmosphere of hydrogen, helium, and methane gases. The upper deck of this atmosphere is seen from space as the planet's cloud tops.

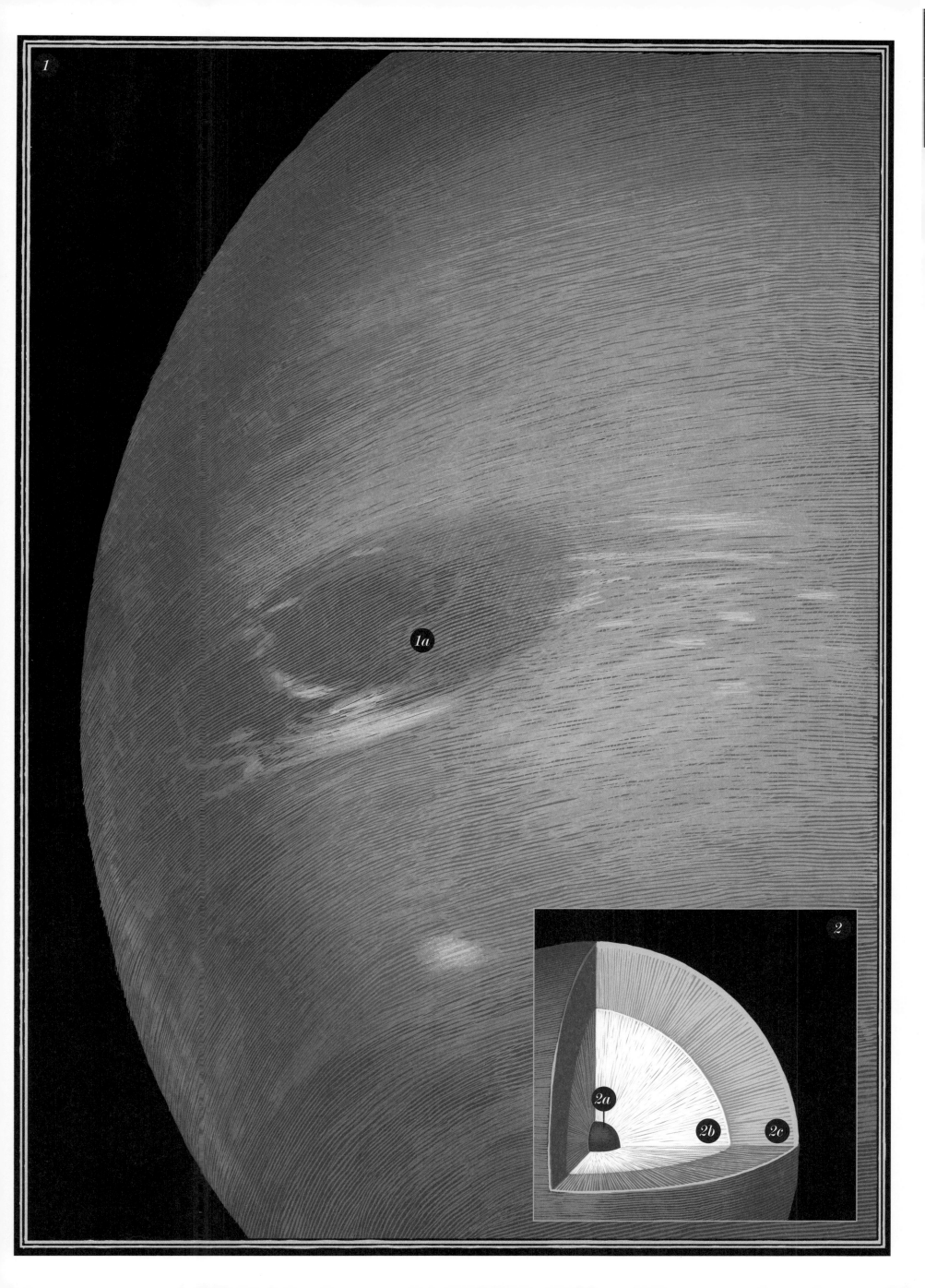

Dwarf Planets

Around and beyond the orbits of the eight planets, the solar system is crowded with other objects: from chips of ice and rock no larger than a fist to objects as big as the planets themselves. So what makes a planet a planet? In 2006, astronomers answered this question and set out three criteria that all planets must meet. First, a planet must be in orbit around the sun. Second, it should have enough mass and gravity to pull itself into a spherical shape. Third, its path around the sun must be clear of other objects. For many years, astronomers classified Pluto as a planet. But while it meets the first two criteria, it fails on the third count, because it shares its neighborhood with other icy objects. So in 2006, its seventy-six-year stint as the smallest planet in the solar system came to an end, and Pluto was given the new label of dwarf planet.

Astronomers think there could be dozens of dwarf planets beyond Pluto's distant orbit, but so far we have identified just five dwarf planets in the solar system. As well as Pluto, we know of Ceres, Eris, Makemake, and Haumea. Most of these are located in the Kuiper Belt, stretching from Neptune's orbit to around 9 billion miles/15 billion kilometers from the sun. But much closer to us is Ceres, the largest object in the asteroid belt between Jupiter and Mars. It was long considered to be an asteroid and was in fact the first "asteroid" ever discovered. However, it was reclassified as a dwarf planet in March 2006, and it was the first dwarf planet to be visited by a spacecraft when NASA's Dawn mission its orbit in 2015.

In July 2015, the New Horizons spacecraft made the first flyby of Pluto, nine years and 3 billion miles/4.8 billion kilometers after the probe was launched. Swooping just 7,800 miles/12,500 kilometers above Pluto's surface, it sent back images that showed an amazing variety of surface features such as craters, cliffs, valleys, and layers of nitrogen ice.

Key to plate

1: **Dwarf planets**

The known dwarf planets are shown to scale alongside Earth. They are in fact great distances apart, mainly in the outer solar system. Since dwarf planets do not have well-established parameters, the figures below may vary.

a) **Pluto (with Charon)**

Diameter: 1,475 miles/2,374 kilometers
Orbital period (year): 248 years
Rotation period (day): 6.4 days
Distance from the sun: 29.6–49.3 AU
Charon is the largest of Pluto's moons.

b) **Eris**

Diameter: 1,491 miles/2,400 kilometers
Orbital period (year): 560.9 years
Rotation period (day): 1.1 days
Distance from the sun: 38.3–97.5 AU

c) **Haumea**

Diameter: 1,218 miles/1,960 kilometers (longest side)
Orbital period (year): 283.3 years
Rotation period (day): 0.2 days
Distance from the sun: 34.7–51.5 AU

d) **Makemake**

Diameter: 889 miles/1,430 kilometers
Orbital period (year): 306 years
Rotation period (day): 0.3 days
Distance from the sun: 38.1–52.8 AU

e) **Ceres**

Diameter: 588 miles/946 kilometers
Orbital period (year): 4.6 years
Rotation period (day): 0.4 days
Distance from the sun: 2.6–3.0 AU

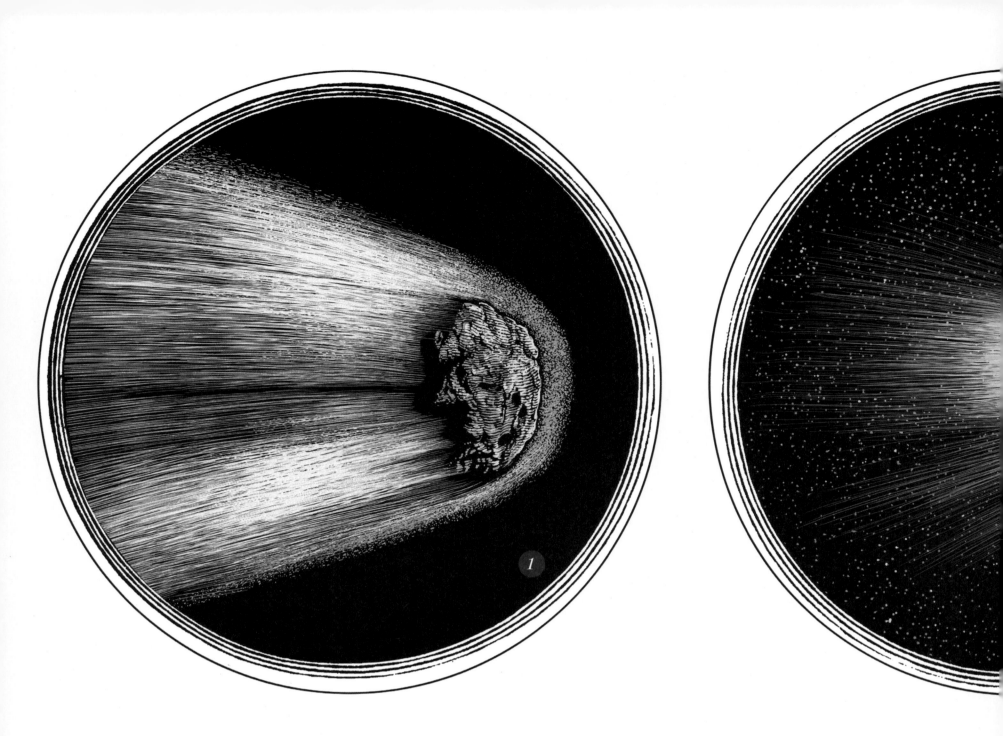

Comets and Asteroids

Comets and asteroids can be thought of as the solar system's "leftovers"—the material that remained after the sun, the planets, and their moons all formed around 4.6 billion years ago. These objects orbit the sun on oval paths, sometimes straying perilously close to the planets, or even careering into them. But apart from this, comets and asteroids are very different from each other in their composition and behavior.

Comets are compact balls of ice and dust, like huge dirty snowballs barreling through space. They begin their journey in the farthest reaches of the solar system, originating in the Kuiper Belt (some 2.3 billion to 9.3 billion miles/4.5 billion to 15 billion kilometers from the sun) or the Oort cloud (a distant 4.7 trillion miles/7.5 trillion kilometers from the sun). As their course brings them closer to the sun, they begin to warm up, and some of their ice turns into vapor. This forms a thick cloud, or coma, of gas and dust around the comet's core. The solar wind (see page 20) "blows" some of this back, and the result is a brilliant tail streaming behind the comet. The largest comets have tails millions of kilometers long and bright enough even to be seen from Earth.

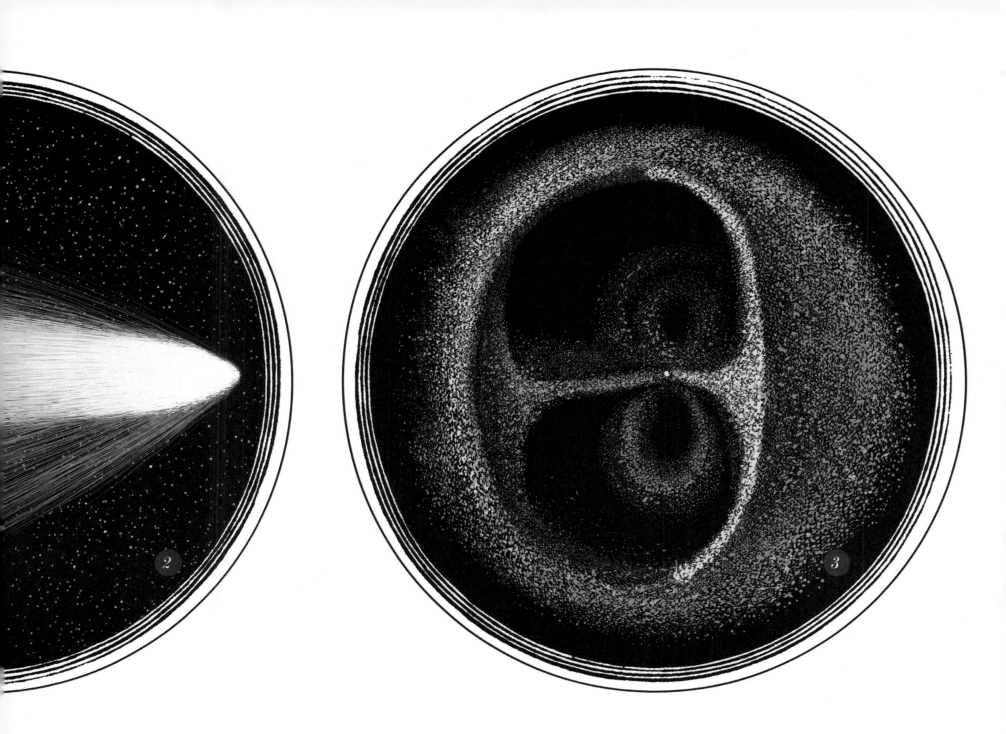

In contrast, asteroids are made of metals and rocky material and have irregular shapes, often resembling potatoes. This is a result of collisions with other objects, after which their gravity is not strong enough to pull them back into a spherical shape. The largest asteroids orbit the sun in a region between Mars and Jupiter known as the asteroid belt, but collisions can knock an asteroid off its path and send it hurtling into the wider solar system.

Many smaller pieces of debris and dust also drift through the solar system. Sometimes pea-size pieces of this interplanetary material enter Earth's upper atmosphere and burn up. We see these as meteors or "shooting stars"—beautiful, bright trails streaking across the sky. Any debris that enters our atmosphere is known as a meteoroid. But if it survives its fall through the atmosphere, it is known as a meteorite. These range from pebble-size lumps to boulders weighing more than 22 tons/20 metric tons.

--- *Key to plate* ---

1: Comet core
The core, or nucleus, of a comet is a fragile, spongelike structure of ice and dust, loosely held together by gravity. It is surrounded by a fuzzy cloud of particles and gases known as a coma, which shines owing to sunlight.

2: Comet tails
As a comet nears the sun, two tails stretch away from it. A white tail forms from dust particles, which sunlight pushes into a curved shape. A blue tail forms as ultraviolet light rips electrons off the coma's atoms, and the solar wind carries away the ionized gas.

3: Oort cloud
The Oort cloud is a halo of icy debris surrounding the solar system. When stars pass close to it, their gravity stirs the cloud so that dormant comets can hurtle out of it toward the inner solar system. Seen here, the sun and all its planets lie within the yellow dot at the center of the cloud.

Exoplanets

Using powerful telescopes and advanced methods, astronomers have discovered incredible worlds beyond our solar system. These faraway planets, or exoplanets, are orbiting distant stars, just like our planet orbits the sun. Of the two hundred billion stars in the Milky Way, scientists estimate twenty billion could have planets of their own.

More than 3,500 exoplanets have been confirmed so far. These range from huge gas giants hugging their star to rocky "super-Earths" nearly the mass of Neptune. Most intriguing of all are Earthlike exoplanets, some of which may even have conditions habitable for life. As we know it, life depends on liquid water and a fixed range of temperatures, so astronomers are looking for planets just the right distance from their star so they are neither too hot nor too cold. These "Goldilocks planets" will be studied for signs of oxygen, ozone, and methane. If found, they could be a sign that we are not alone in the universe.

However, finding an exoplanet in the first place is not an easy task. That's because the glare from a star can outshine its planet by up to a billion times, making exoplanets impossible to photograph through a telescope. Astronomers therefore use less direct methods, searching for signals that may indicate the presence of a distant exoplanet. One technique is the radial velocity method: this draws on the fact that an orbiting planet's gravity will always make its star wobble a little bit. For instance, the sun wobbles back and forth due to gravitational tugs mainly from Jupiter and Saturn. By measuring the wobble of a star, astronomers can work out the mass of its planets, a bit like watching someone walk an exuberant dog: if you're so far away that you can see the owner but not the dog, you can tell the dog is there—and guess how big it is—by watching the owner be pulled along!

Another way of finding exoplanets is called transiting, whereby starlight as we see it can appear slightly dimmed if a planet moves across the star's face. It is only a very tiny effect, however. Imagine finding a firefly crawling over a searchlight by measuring a dimming of the searchlight's brightness—and doing that from 620 miles/1,000 kilometers away. But still, astronomers can use this method to carefully measure a star's changes in brightness and determine the size and orbits of its exoplanets.

Key to plate

1: **55 Cancri e (aka Janssen)**
The super-Earth exoplanet known as 55 Cancri e (or Janssen) has a diameter twice that of our planet. Located about 40 light-years away toward the constellation of Cancer, the exoplanet is orbiting so close to its sunlike star, 55 Cancri A, that its dayside temperatures can reach between 1,832°F and 4,892°F/1,000°C and 2,700°C. It is thought to be an extremely hostile environment, covered in lava flows, with molten plumes of gas and dust sometimes engulfing the whole planet. Scientists think this super-hot planet may have a thick atmosphere that hasn't been stripped away by the radiation from its star.

The Sun

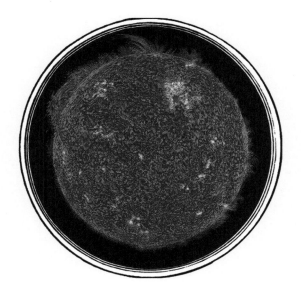

The Sun

The Sun-Earth Connection

The Death of the Sun

The Sun

At the center of our solar system is the sun, an ordinary star that has been shining for 4.56 billion years. Like all stars, it is a hot ball of densely squeezed hydrogen and helium gases, which are so hot that they exist in a state of matter known as plasma: a high-temperature mix of electrons and ions (atoms that have lost electrons). Shining with the energy of 100 billion tons of dynamite exploding every second, the sun is by far the most powerful object in our solar system. It is also the largest: its diameter is almost a hundred times greater than Earth's, and it contains a staggering 99.86 percent of all the mass in the solar system. This gives it a powerful gravitational field, holding in orbit everything around it, from the biggest planets to the smallest rocks.

The sun's great density means we have no way of seeing its innermost layers, so everything we know about its interior comes from close observation of its surface. For instance, astronomers listen to the "music" of the sun by studying the sound waves that bounce inside it. The reflection of these sound waves makes the sun's surface pulse very slightly, and the rising and falling of this layer can be measured to give information about conditions inside the sun. From this, we know that the sun has many different layers.

The sun does not have clear boundaries in its interior like Earth does. Instead, it gradually changes in density and temperature through six main zones. The temperature of its plasma increases from around 11,000°F/6,000°C at the upper visible layer to 27 million°F/15 million°C at its innermost region (the core). In the core, the strong force of gravity squeezes the sun's hydrogen atoms to a density thirteen times greater than that of lead. In such extreme conditions, hydrogen fuses together to form helium. This process, known as nuclear fusion, releases enormous amounts of energy—and that energy powers the sun and makes it shine.

Key to plate

1: Layers of the sun

a) The core, the innermost part of the sun, extends from the center to about 25 percent of the solar radius.
b) The radiative zone, through which the core's heat travels and cools to around 3.6 million°F/2 million°C.
c) The convective zone, which transports energy outward as bubbles of gas, roiling like a boiling kettle.
d) The photosphere: the 250-mile-/400-kilometer-thick visible surface of the sun. Sunlight emerges here and travels into space.
e) The chromosphere, which cannot easily be seen due to the brilliant flood of light from the photosphere.
f) The corona, the sun's outermost atmosphere—a thinly spread gas that ranges from 1.7 million°F/1 million°C to more than 17 million°F/10 million°C.

2: Coronal loops

Coronal loops can extend between 1,600 and 62,000 miles/2,500 and 100,000 kilometers above the surface of the sun. The loops are magnetic tubes filled with hot gas and anchored at both ends into the photosphere.

3: Solar flares

These eruptions occur around highly magnetic and active regions of the sun. The largest (X-class) flares can blast out an energy equivalent to a million hydrogen bombs exploding on Earth at the same time.

4: Sunspots

These temporary spots appear dark because they are cooler than the surrounding photosphere. Sunspots can be as large as Earth and move across the sun's surface as it rotates.

The Sun-Earth Connection

Life on Earth can only exist because our planet lies at the perfect distance from the sun. From around 93 million miles/150 million kilometers away, the sun provides the amount of heat and light necessary for liquid water, plants, fossil fuels, and a moderate climate to exist on our planet. If the sun were any farther away we would freeze; if it were closer we would boil. Crucially, the sun also has enough energy to shine for billions of years. But it's not just the sun's light and heat that impact us. There is also a close connection between explosive changes on the sun and disturbances in the space environment around Earth. These fluctuations can be thought of as "space weather" around our planet.

Although the sun might look the same to us from one day to another, it is in fact undergoing constant changes. Every eleven years, there is a peak in the energetic events on its surface—a pattern of activity known as the solar cycle. During solar maximum, when activity is at its highest, the surface of the sun is regularly marked by dark sunspots and powerful explosions. One of the most violent explosions is a solar flare, whereby energy stored in magnetic fields is suddenly released in a burst of radiation and electrically charged particles. Another dramatic event is the coronal mass ejection (CME), whereby bubbles of plasma are blown away from the sun over a few hours. The average CME colliding with the Earth can inject an additional 1,500 gigawatts of electricity into the atmosphere — almost twice the power generation capability of the entire United States!

The matter expelled in flares and CMEs usually reaches Earth within two to four days of leaving the sun, carried through the solar system by the solar wind (see page 20). When the fast-moving particles approach our planet, they accelerate along its magnetic field and enter the upper atmosphere. The solar particles then collide with atmospheric gas atoms, causing them to give off a shimmer of colored light. These are seen as the lights of the aurora borealis, flickering in the night skies over Earth's magnetic poles. They are the most visible sign of the space weather made by our dynamic star.

Key to plate

1: **Magnetic fields**
Earth's magnetic field creates a "magnetosphere" around the planet, shielding it from particles released by the sun. This steady flow of particles (forming the solar wind) compresses Earth's magnetosphere on the dayside and stretches it into a long tail on the nightside. Most of the solar wind is thus deflected, but when a solar storm such as a CME strikes Earth, it strikes the magnetosphere. The magnetic field is slightly peeled open, allowing high-energy particles to enter the atmosphere over the magnetic poles — seen as the aurora borealis.

2: **Solar eclipse**
A total eclipse of the sun occurs when the moon passes in front of the sun and entirely covers its face. This is only possible because the moon is 400 times smaller than the sun and the sun is 400 times farther away than the moon—a unique coincidence within the solar system. Sometimes the moon only blocks a part of the sun, and we see a partial or annular eclipse.

3: **The sun's corona**
During a total eclipse, the moment when the moon completely obscures the sun is known as "totality." At this point we can see the shimmering white light of the solar corona around a magnificent circle of black.

THE SUN

The Death of the Sun

Stars are not eternal: they are born, they live, and then they die. Our sun is no different from any other star in this respect, and it can only shine for as long as it has a source of energy. At present, the sun gets its energy by converting 700 million tons/635 million metric tons of hydrogen in its core into 695 million tons/630 million metric tons of helium every second, in the process of nuclear fusion. But once all the hydrogen in its core has been fused into helium, the sun will start to run out of fuel. Its death will have a devastating impact on the solar system.

Today, almost 4.6 billion years since its birth, the sun is about halfway through its life—you could say its fuel tank is half-empty. About 5 billion years from now, nuclear fusion will no longer be possible in the sun's interior, marking the beginning of the end for our star. Once the sun has converted almost all the hydrogen in its core,

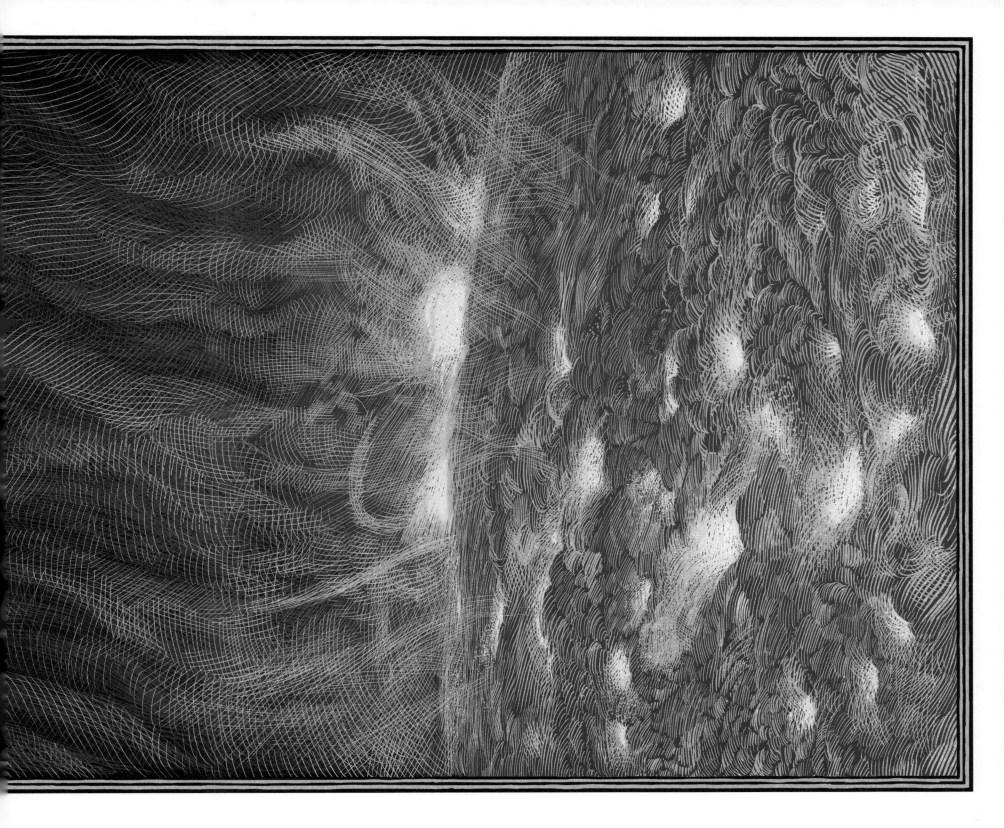

it will begin converting the hydrogen in its outer layers. This means it will carry on shining—but with its core no longer active, it will start to collapse under its own gravity. The pressure of this contraction will release additional energy and heat, making the sun swell in size to a huge red giant star. At this stage, astronomers predict the sun will be almost three hundred times its present size. Mercury and Venus will have been swallowed up, and though Earth might just escape this fate, the sun's fierce heat will still scorch our planet. However, the sun's death will also change the boundary of the habitable zone in the solar system. While Earth will no longer be habitable, much of the outer solar system will become warmer. Formerly icy worlds will melt, and liquid water will be present on their surface. It is even possible that the dwarf planet Eris will become our new home.

Key to plate

1: **Red giant sun**

Billions of years from now, when the sun grows into a red giant, astronomers predict it will engulf Mercury and Venus, but they are not sure what will happen to Earth.

Even if the sun's swelling stops before it reaches us, its proximity and fierce heat will burn our planet. Its red form will fill half the sky, the oceans will boil off in the heat, and all life will cease to exist as Earth turns into a

molten rocky body. However, that day is still billions of years into the future, meaning humans have plenty of time to develop the technology we need to leave Earth and find a new home.

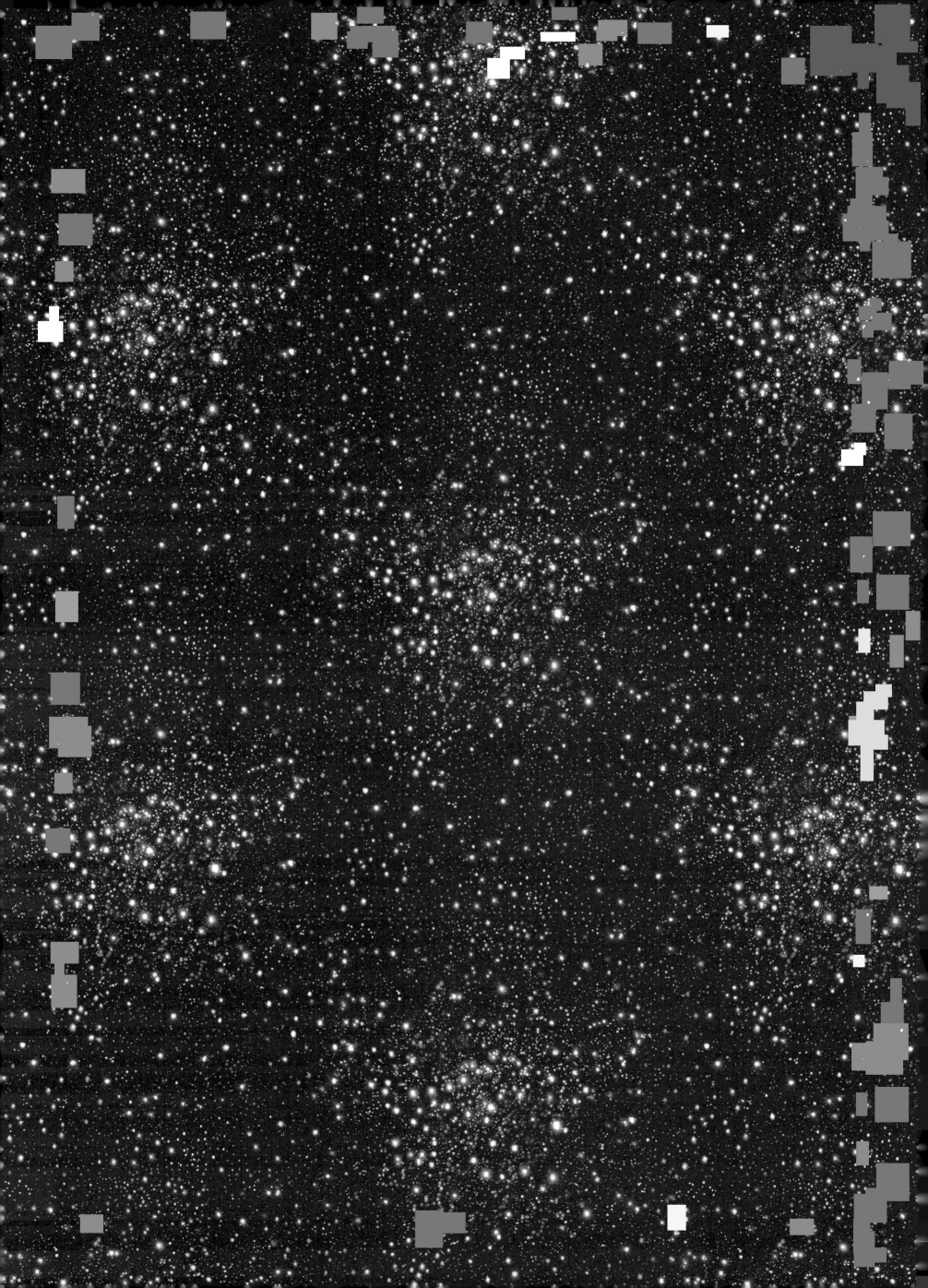

The Night Sky

The Night Sky
Northern Hemisphere Constellations
Southern Hemisphere Constellations

The Night Sky

A dark starry sky is one of the most glorious wonders of nature. On a clear, moonless night, away from the glare of city lights, we can see about two thousand sparkling stars with the unaided eye. Even without any equipment, we can start to observe certain properties of the stars, and most people should be able to notice three main features.

First, stars are not all the same brightness. They differ greatly in size and power output, and the most powerful stars emit more light than others, meaning they appear brighter from a distance. Some stars also appear brighter from Earth because they are nearer to our planet—the sun is of course the ultimate example of this.

Second, stars aren't all the same color. While most appear white, some have a reddish, blue, or yellow hue. These colors reveal the stars' different surface temperatures: hotter stars look blue, whereas cooler ones look red. Be careful not to confuse the hints of star colors with more visibly colorful planets. Mercury, Venus, Mars, Jupiter, and Saturn can all be seen with the naked eye: Mercury has a yellow hue; Venus looks silvery; Mars is the "red planet"; Jupiter appears whitish; and Saturn is creamy

yellow. These objects, which reflect the sun's light, usually appear brighter in the sky than stars, but they do not twinkle.

Third, the stars are not evenly spread across the sky. Some of the brighter stars seem to cluster in groups, forming shapes that we call constellations. Despite appearing to be connected, the stars in a constellation usually have no relation to one another: they can be vast distances apart and form shapes by chance because of how they align in our sky. All the stars are gradually moving in different orbits (though their great distance from Earth means it takes a long time for us to notice this motion), which means that a few hundred thousand years from now the stars will have moved so much that the patterns they make will have changed completely. Night sky watchers of the distant future will have to make up whole new constellations!

Key to plate

1: **View of the night sky**
Besides the stars, the night can also be decorated with other beautiful sights. At certain times of the year we can see our Milky Way galaxy (see page 76) as a magnificent arc of stars

stretching across the sky. The faint band of light seen from Earth gives the galaxy a "milky" appearance after which it is named.

During the year you can also look out for displays of meteor showers.

Spectacular showers that can be seen from the northern and southern hemispheres include Orionids (late October), Leonids (November), Geminids (mid-December), and Lyrids (mid-April).

Northern Hemisphere Constellations

Since ancient times, humans have seen patterns in the stars. Tracing shapes between the brightest points, they imagined gods and heroes, wild creatures and mythical beasts: apparent shapes known as constellations. As the constellations were named after the shapes they most resembled, distant civilizations occasionally "shared" the same figures. For example, the constellation the Greeks named Orion the hunter was seen by the ancient Chinese as a supreme hunter or warrior named Shen. This pattern was also associated with the Egyptian pharaoh Unas, and in Hungary is seen as a magical archer. In other cases, different cultures have seen totally opposing shapes in the same star pattern. For instance, the seven brightest stars within the Ursa Major constellation are recognized as a variety of forms: in the U.K. it is called the Plough; in the United States it is the Big Dipper; in France it is known as a saucepan; to the ancient Maya it was a mythological parrot; Hindu folklore called it the Seven Rishis (or Wise Men); and the ancient Chinese thought of it as a special chariot for the Emperor of Heaven.

By the early twentieth century, there were so many constellations in use that the International Astronomical Union (IAU) officially assigned eighty-eight constellations across the northern and southern skies. These official constellations have exactly fitting boundaries like jigsaw pieces so that every place in the sky belongs within one. They have a practical purpose today, as astronomers use constellations to divide the sky into regions for placing the location of objects. The most visible stars are named after the constellation they appear in, and are further labeled using the Greek alphabet to show how bright they are. For example, Beta Orionis is named after *beta*, the second letter in the Greek alphabet, and Orion, the constellation. This tells us it is the second brightest star in Orion.

One of the most prominent stars in the northern sky is Polaris (also known as the North Star or polestar, and technically designated Alpha Ursae Minoris). Although it is only about the fiftieth-brightest star, it is uniquely useful to navigators as it stays almost completely still in our sky. This happens because Polaris is located at the north celestial pole, the point around which the northern sky seems to turn. Consequently, it can always be used to find the way north!

Key to plate

1: **Northern hemisphere constellations**

This star chart is typical of those used by astronomers in the sixteenth to the eighteenth centuries. Not only were the charts tools for navigation and study, they also became objects of great beauty in themselves. Although the illustrations may have little to do with modern science, they are part of astronomy's cultural heritage.

Many classical mythological forms are depicted in this northern hemisphere chart. For instance, the image of a lion appears among the stars of the constellation Leo. Meanwhile, the mythical creature known as Pegasus, depicted as a horse with wings, can be seen in the lower-right corner of the chart.

Southern Hemisphere Constellations

The southern hemisphere offers some of the best stargazing opportunities in the world. Here, the graceful curve of the Milky Way can be seen stretching from horizon to horizon, and this is the only place where we can glimpse two of our neighboring galaxies, the Large and Small Magellanic Clouds. The southern hemisphere also boasts the three brightest stars in the night sky: Sirius, Canopus, and Alpha Centauri (the nearest star system to our sun). The star Canopus is part of the famous Carina constellation. This spectacular cluster of around three hundred stars includes the gargantuan star Eta Carina, which will die in a supernova thousands of years from now, and the Carina Nebula, a huge, bright area of space where stars are constantly being born.

The indigenous peoples of Australasia were among the first humans to name objects in the night sky, but the majority of southern constellations adopted by the IAU were mapped out in the sixteenth century by European explorers. During this time, charting the stars was particularly important, as celestial navigation was the only way to navigate away from land. One of the principal constellations for navigation was Crux, or the Southern Cross. Although it is the smallest of the eighty-eight constellations ascribed by the IAU, its four main stars have unusual brightness, and it can be seen all year long. Crux is depicted on several national flags, including those of Australia, New Zealand, Papua New Guinea, Samoa, and Brazil. A particular highlight within Crux is the Jewel Box cluster — when viewed through a telescope, it reveals almost a hundred red and blue stars.

Key to plate

1: **Southern hemisphere constellations**

A prominent constellation in this southern star chart is Centaurus (center right). It is depicted as a centaur: a mythical creature that is a horse from the waist down and a man above the waist. In ancient Greek mythology, Centaurus represented

Chiron, the leader of the centaurs.

One of the oldest documented constellations in the sky, Aquarius, is shown at the ten-o'clock position. Aquarius is the tenth largest constellation, but since there are no particularly bright stars in the constellation, it can be difficult to view in the night sky.

Other highlights in this chart include Hydra in the form of a long, writhing water snake. It is the largest constellation and stretches along the right of the chart with its tail ending between Centaurus and Libra (the "weighing scales"). Running up from the bottom left is the stippled band of the Milky Way.

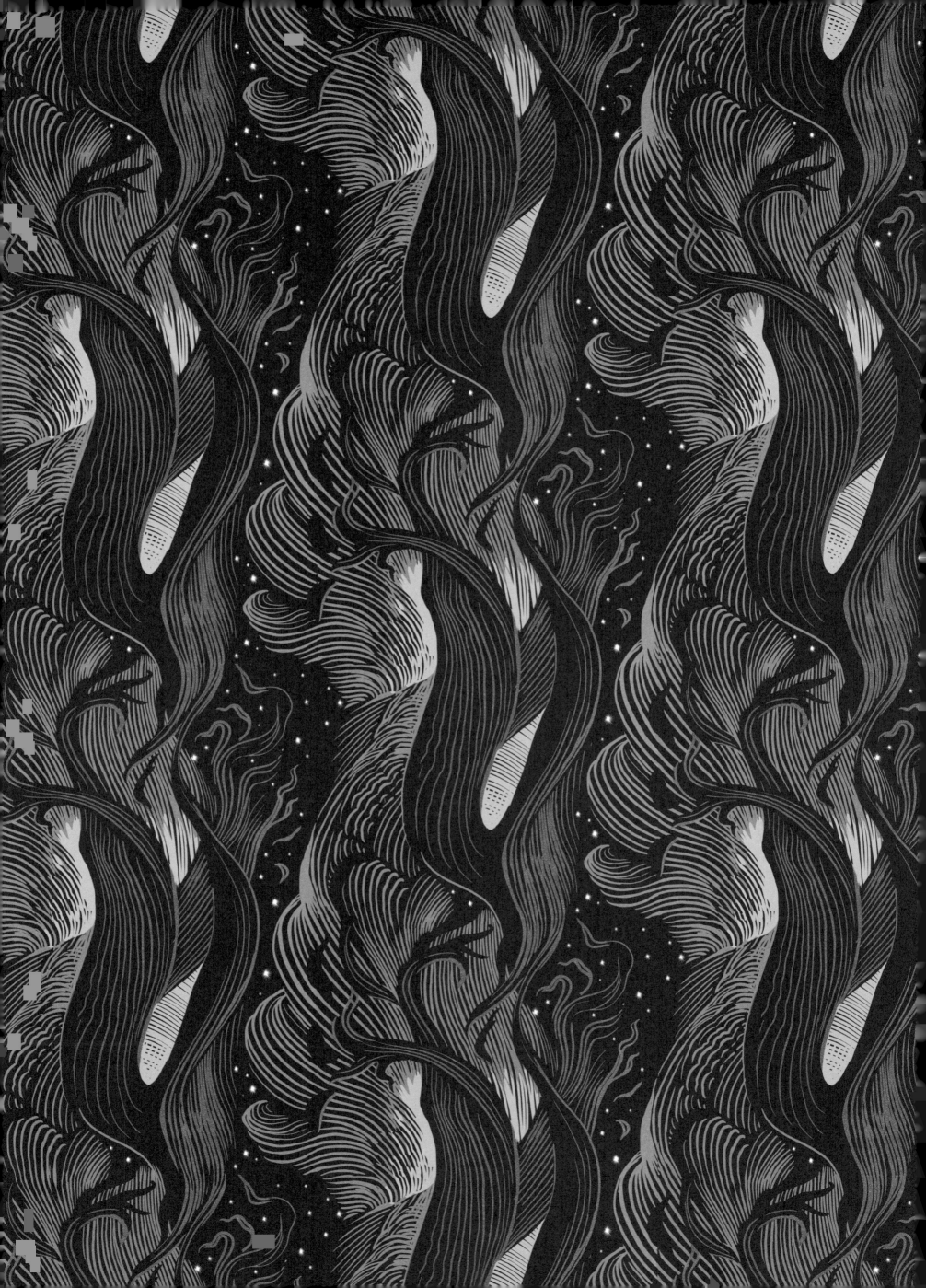

Gallery 5

The Stars

Star Types
Stellar Births
The Life Cycle of Stars
Stellar Deaths
Black Holes

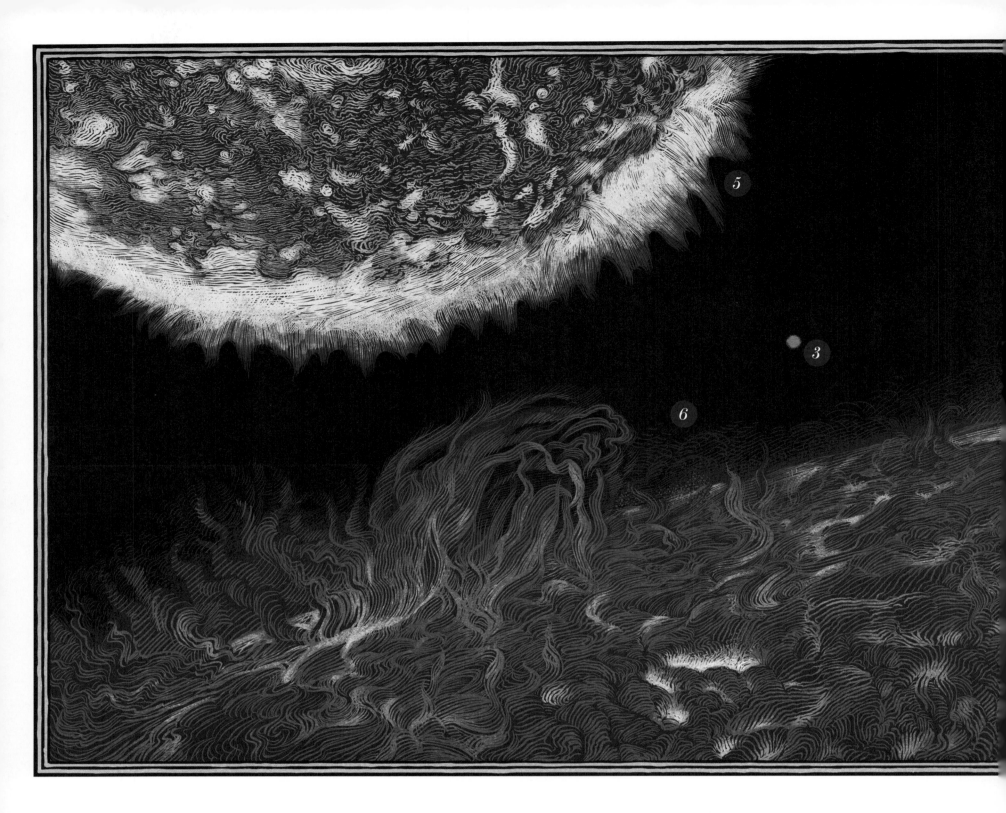

Star Types

The universe contains at least a thousand billion trillion stars, each one a giant glowing ball of gas that generates heat, light, and other types of radiation. From Earth, all stars look fairly similar, but in fact, stars vary enormously in terms of size (diameter), mass (amount of matter), temperature, color, luminosity (power output), and age.

As there are so many different types of stars, scientists have developed several ways of categorizing them. First, they are classed by their temperature, as types O, B, A, F, G, K, or M, in a system devised by astronomer Annie Jump Cannon. Stars are arranged in order of decreasing surface temperature, where O-type stars are the hottest and M-type are the coolest. Stars with different temperatures seem to shine with different colors. The hottest stars appear blue, while the coolest appear red.

Stars are also classed by size, as dwarfs, giants, or supergiants. Our star, the sun, is a G-type dwarf star. But there are even smaller dwarf stars in the universe: the smallest known star is the dwarf EBLM J0555-57Ab, which is only slightly larger than the planet Saturn. In contrast, one of the largest known stars in the universe is the supergiant NML Cygni. It is about 5,300 light-years away from Earth, and is 1,650 times

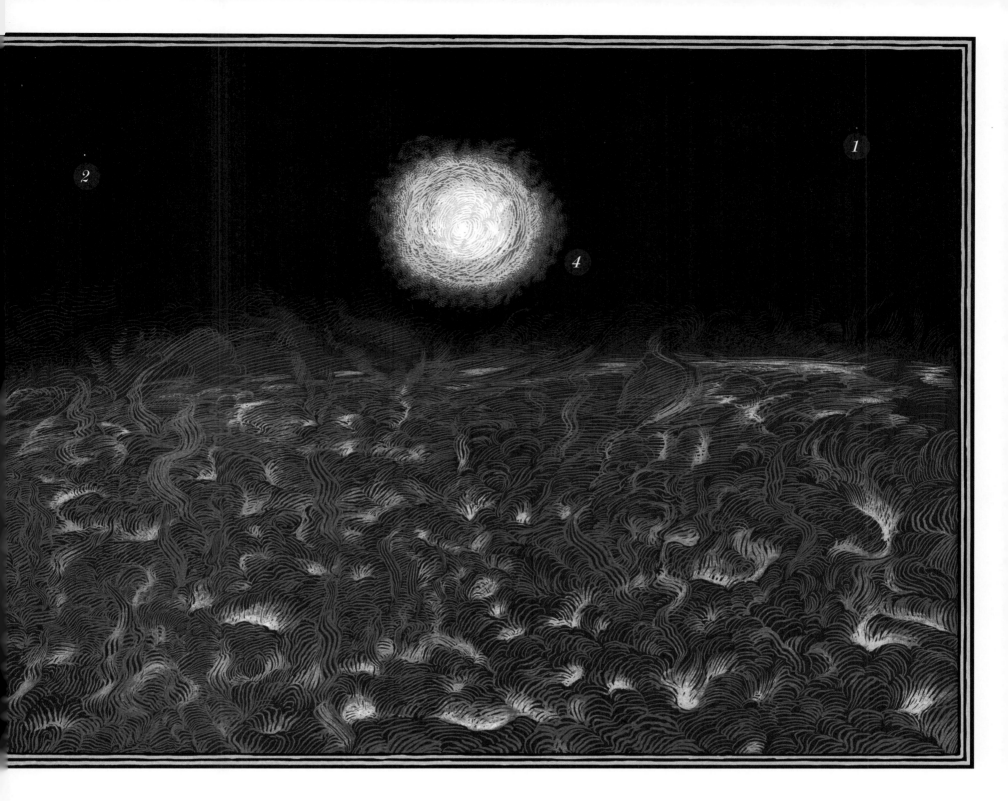

the size of the sun. If it were placed in our sun's position, its surface would stretch beyond the orbit of Jupiter.

As stars all have a life cycle, we can also categorize them by age, from newly born stars to mature, old, and dying stars. The length and shape of each star's life will be determined by its birth mass, with the heaviest stars leading the shortest lives.

Key to plate

1: **Brown dwarf**
Surface temperature:
1,800–3,600°F/1,000–2,000°C
Radius: 0.05–0.12 solar radii
(1 solar radius is 432,300 miles/
695,700 kilometers)
Energy output: 0.00001 times the sun's

2: **White dwarf**
Surface temperature:
7,200–270,000°F/4,000–150,000°C
Radius: 0.008–0.2 solar radii
Energy output: 0.0001–100 times the sun's

3: **Yellow dwarf**
Surface temperature:
9,000–12,600°F/5,000–7,000°C
Radius: 0.96–1.4 solar radii
Energy output: 0.6–5.0 times
the sun's

4: **Red giant**
Surface temperature:
12,600–16,200°F/7,000–9,000°C
Radius: 20–100 solar radii
Energy output: 100–1,000
times the sun's

5: **Blue supergiant**
Surface temperature:
18,000–36,000°F/10,000–20,000°C
Radius: 100–2,000 solar radii
Energy output: 1,000–800,000 times
the sun's

6: **Red supergiant**
Surface temperature:
5,400–9,000°F/3,000–5,000°C
Radius: 100–2,000 solar radii
Energy output: 1,000–800,000 times
the sun's

Stellar Births

All stars have a beginning and a birthplace. They are assembled within beautiful clouds of gas and dust known as nebulae: stellar nurseries that can contain great numbers of new stars. On average, somewhere in our Milky Way galaxy about three new stars are born every year, but some other galaxies have far more prolific star-making factories, forging hundreds or even thousands of stars a year.

Nebulae are mostly formed of hydrogen and helium gas, together with microscopic particles of dust. These clouds may remain undisturbed for millions of years but will leap into star formation if they are disturbed, for instance, by the shock waves of a nearby star exploding. This trigger will cause the cloud to collapse under its own gravity, shrinking in size and spinning faster and faster. The outer parts of it will become disc-shaped, while the innermost region of cloud will be sculpted into a rough sphere. Growing hotter and hotter, the ball will eventually form a glowing core known as a protostar. Because protostars are shrouded in leftover gas and dust from their nebulae, they are very difficult to detect in visible light, so astronomers use infrared telescopes to peer through the dusty veil and glimpse the earliest stages of a star's birth.

About a hundred thousand to a million years after its formation, the protostar will become hot enough to clear away most of the material around it, so it can be seen in visible light. Once its internal temperatures reach around 27 million°F/15 million°C, nuclear fusion reactions are triggered in its core, fusing atoms together to release incredible amounts of energy. This means the star can ignite and finally start to shine.

After their formation, most stars are still surrounded by some of the material from their former nebula. These elements spin in a hot, flat disc around the star, but as the star becomes stable, they will cool down and start to clump together. Over millions of years, these clumps may converge, forming young planets known as planetesimals.

Key to plate

1: **The Orion Nebula**
The Orion Nebula, located almost 1,350 light-years away in the constellation of Orion, is a beautiful example of an active star-forming region. It contains vast numbers of newly forged stars, and their radiation lights up the nebula's structure.

The Orion Nebula spans about 40 light-years and can be seen with the unaided eye from very dark locations on Earth. The whole nebula will slowly disperse over the next hundred thousand years, owing to the radiation and matter flowing out of it from powerful, newly formed stars.

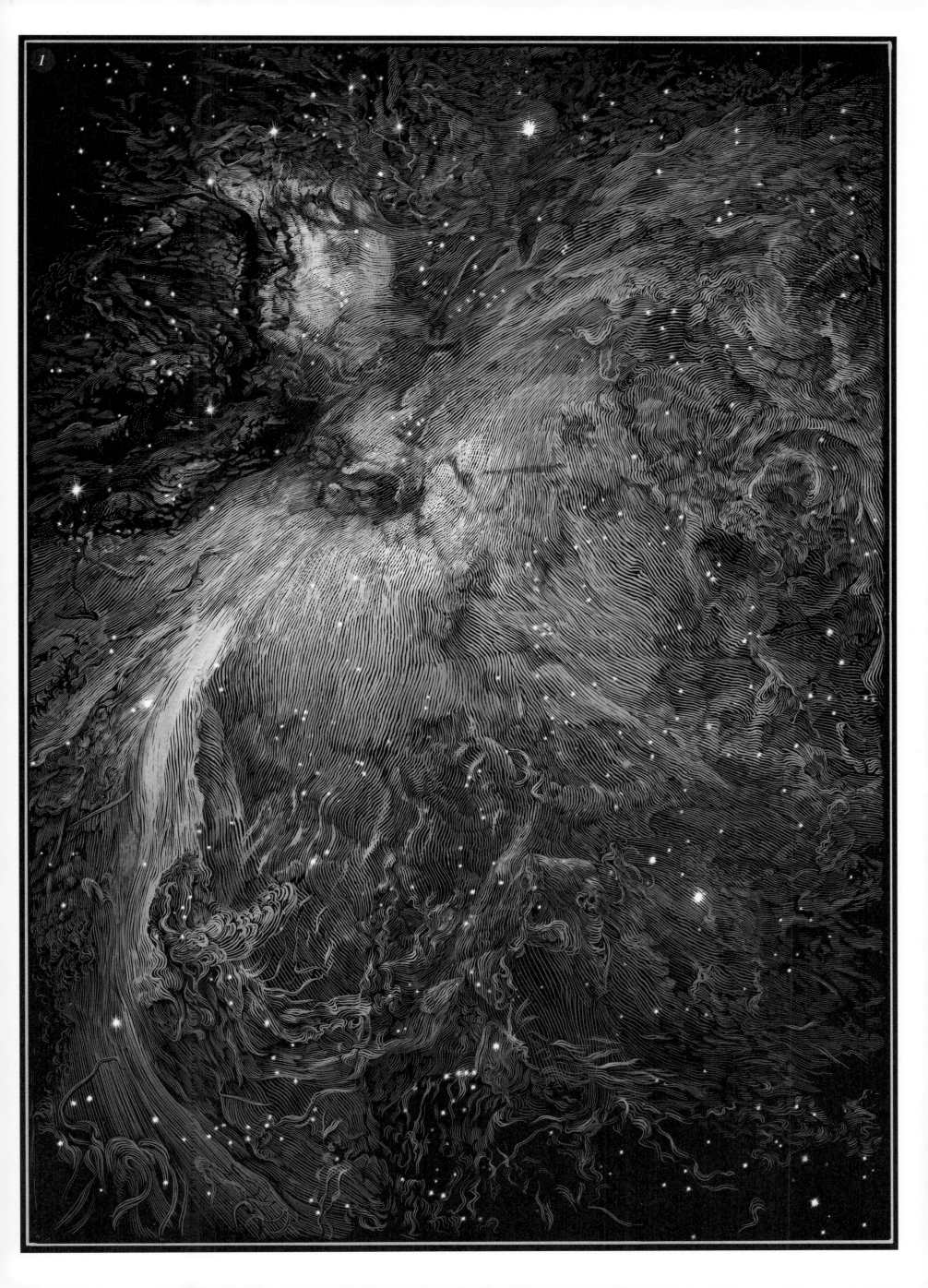

The Life Cycle of Stars

During its life, every star is locked in a battle between the gravity pushing inward on it and the pressure of hot gases in its interior pushing outward. When the two forces are balanced, the star is stable. However, there comes a time in every star's life when its supply of fuel runs out: it stops making energy, gravity takes over, and the star enters the final stages of its life. This happens to all stars, but the timing and manner of a star's death will be determined by its mass at birth. Broadly, we can think of stars as either "lightweight," "middleweight," or "heavyweight," and each type has its own unique life cycle.

Lightweight stars are born with masses 0.8 to 8 times the mass of the sun. These stars spend several billion years in a stable phase, making energy by converting hydrogen to helium. When all their hydrogen fuel is exhausted, lightweight stars balloon outward and become red giants. A few million years later, their outer layers puff out into space in a planetary nebula. All that will remain of the star after this is a core compressed by gravity to about the size of Earth. This stellar corpse is called a white dwarf star.

Middleweight stars start off with masses eight to twenty times the mass of the sun. They evolve much faster than sunlike stars, barely spending a billion years in their stable phase before they use up their nuclear fuel supply. They then evolve into vast supergiants that emit an enormous amount of light. The death of these huge stars is triggered by a violent supernova explosion, lifting away all the outer layers of the star. All that remains after the explosion is an incredibly dense, city-size core known as a neutron star.

The most massive (heavyweight) stars are more than twenty times the mass of the sun. In just a few million years they consume all their available fuel through the fusion reactions in their core. At this point, the stars rapidly swell into enormous blue supergiants, then just as quickly collapse in the lead-up to a supernova detonation. The life cycle of heavyweight stars ends with the formation of a black hole.

Key to plate

1: **Interstellar nebula**
All stars are born inside a nebula when the cloud of gas collapses.

2: **Protostar**
Gas spins around the star as it forms, making a wide disc of stellar material.

3: **Lightweight star life cycle**
a) The star enters the main sequence, where the balance between its gravity and outward force is equal. While in the main sequence, the star generates energy from the fusion of hydrogen into helium. It is stable for a few billion years.
b) The star becomes a red giant when it runs out of hydrogen in its core. Its core collapses as its external layers swell outward.
c) Its outer layers are shed in a planetary nebula.
d) All that remains is the shrunken core, known as a white dwarf.

4: **Middleweight star life cycle**
a) The star enters the main sequence. It burns its fuel very quickly.
b) When the star runs out of fuel, it expands into a red supergiant.
c) The star explodes as a supernova.
d) All that remains is a very dense core called a neutron star.

5: **Heavyweight star life cycle**
a) The star enters the main sequence.
b) When the star runs out of fuel, it expands into a huge blue supergiant.
c) The star explodes as a supernova.
d) If the star remnant is above 3 solar masses (three times the size of the sun), the remnant becomes a black hole.

Stellar Deaths

After lightweight, middleweight, and heavyweight stars have completed their life cycles, they leave behind three main end states: white dwarfs, neutron stars, and black holes. These are some of the strangest objects in space, where matter is held in the most extreme conditions known to us.

Most stars in the universe are lightweight stars, and all of them will end their lives as white dwarfs. These dense objects contain around a sun's worth of mass crushed into a ball the size of the Earth. At this density, even the electrons in atoms are pushed together, and a teaspoon of white dwarf matter would weigh 5.5 tons/5 metric tons on Earth. As a white dwarf cools down over millions of years, the carbon in its core slowly crystalizes to make diamond. Over billions of years, these huge "diamonds in the sky" cool and fade to become black dwarf stars that emit no light at all.

Neutron stars are formed after the detonation of a massive star in a supernova explosion. In this extreme case, the force of gravity crushes the giant star down into a ball of neutrons (particles with no charge) barely 6 miles/10 kilometers across. It is so much denser than a white dwarf that a teaspoon of neutron star matter would weigh 11 million tons/10 million metric tons on Earth! Because the star is squeezed by so much pressure, it ends up spinning incredibly fast (more than fifty times per second) and having an extremely strong magnetic field.

When the most massive stars die in a supernova explosion, the object left behind may be more than five times the mass of the sun. There is no known force that can hold this object up, so it collapses to the most remarkable of end states: a black hole.

Key to plate

1: The Crab Nebula today

The Crab Nebula is left over from a star dying in a huge supernova. The explosion was first witnessed on Earth in 1054. What we can see today is the hot gas that was propelled into space by the blast.

The nebula spans about 10 light-years across and contains a rich range of chemical elements that were forged inside the star before it died. These elements will eventually be dispersed into space to become the raw materials for making the next generation of stars and planets.

2: The formation of the Crab Nebula

a) **Supernova explosion**

The massive star rapidly collapses under gravity, then rebounds off its hard stellar core. The shock wave that results travels out at speeds of almost 124 million miles per hour/200 million kilometers per hour.

b) **The aftermath of the explosion**

The supernova's shock wave slams into clouds of gas and dust released by the star some twenty thousand years before it died. The shock wave heats up the rings of material and causes them to glow.

c) **The supernova remnant**

Several hundred years after the star explodes, its gas and dust continue to spread outward into space. In time, this gas will form new nebulae and be turned into brand-new stars.

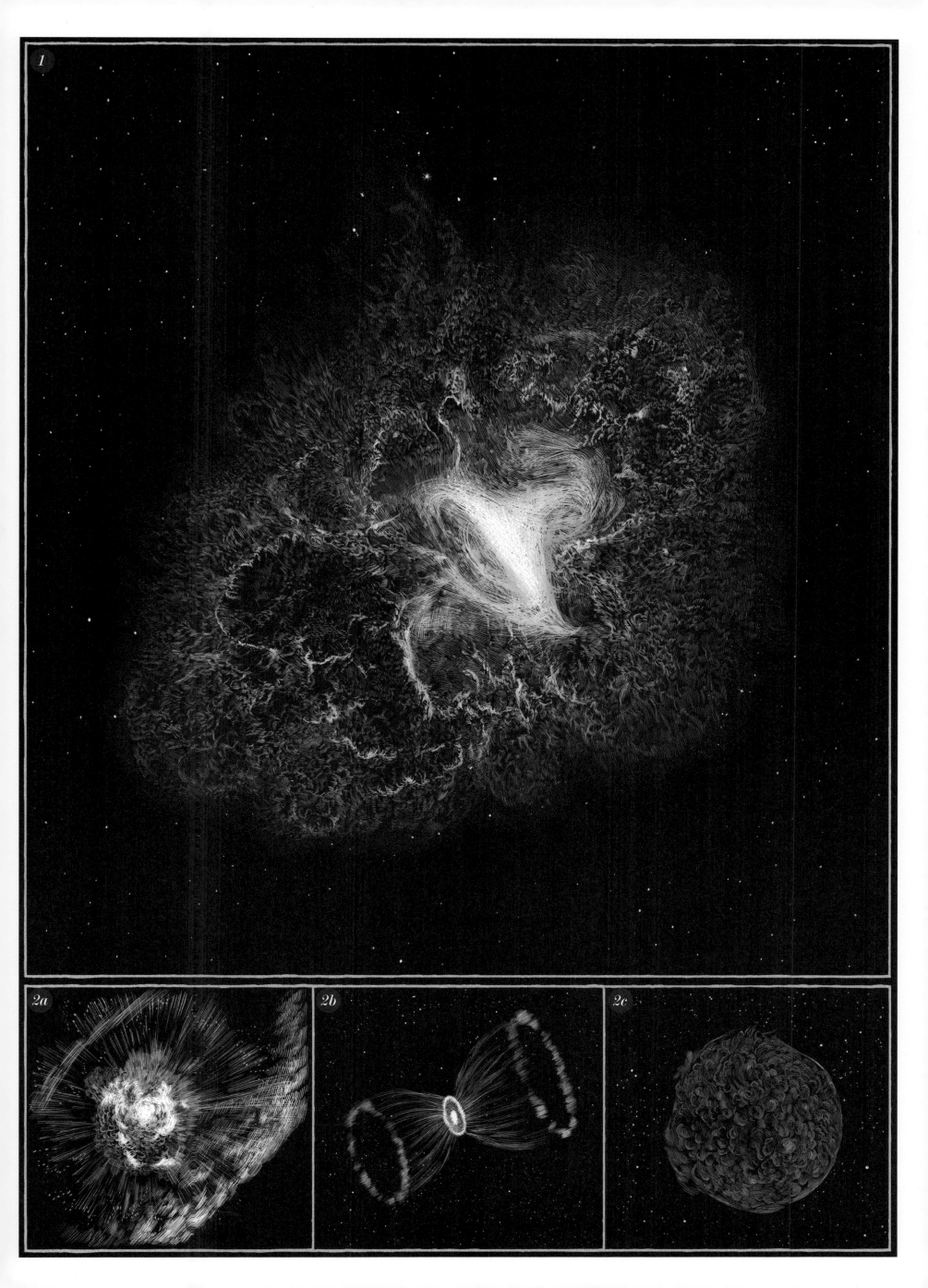

Black Holes

Black holes are among the most fascinating and mysterious objects in the universe. They can't be seen, but if a human got too close to one, they would be sucked in by its gravitational pull, stretched out like spaghetti, and incinerated in a wall of fire! The same fate would befall any object, from a planet to a star, that crossed the outer boundary or "event horizon" of a black hole. After that, there is no going back.

A black hole is formed when a massive star (more than twenty times the mass of the sun) burns through the last of its fuel, collapses, and explodes as a supernova. In this case, the core left behind is too massive to form a comparatively stable neutron star. Instead, the core (up to five times the mass of the sun) collapses into an incredibly dense region: a black hole is formed. Because it is so massive and spinning so fast, the black hole warps the space around it so that nothing, not even light, can escape from it.

Although black holes have an uncommonly strong gravitational pull, they are not like giant vacuum cleaners sucking up the universe. Only matter that gets very close to them is trapped by their gravity and the warped space around them. For example, if the sun was replaced by a black hole of the same mass, Earth would not fall into it. Only objects that came within 2 miles/3 kilometers would be pulled in by its gravity.

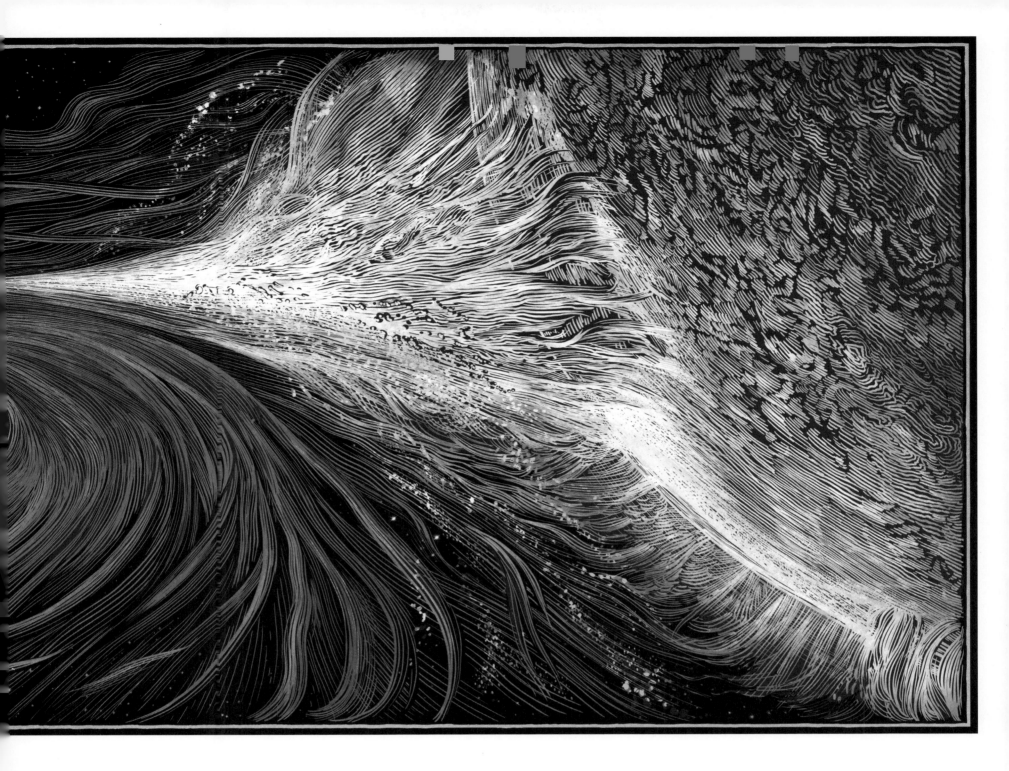

Black holes don't emit or reflect any light, which makes them completely invisible. However, scientists can tell they are there by studying the influence that they have on very nearby stars. This is possible because many stars are not alone in space, but are born in pairs (known as binaries). At the end of their lives, one of the stars in the pair may end as a black hole, while the other remains a normal star. We might then see the normal star orbiting an invisible object. This tells us it must be moving around a black hole.

Scientists have also detected a special kind of wave known as a gravitational wave, which is released when two black holes crash together. This collision creates a "ripple" in space that can be measured on Earth using giant detectors such as those at the Laser Interferometer Gravitational-Wave Observatory (LIGO) in the United States. The shape and size of ripples detected tell us that there are black holes more than twenty times the mass of the sun crashing into each other somewhere in the universe.

Key to plate

1: **A black hole**

When a black hole and an ordinary star are orbiting each other as a pair, matter can be pulled off the ordinary star by the gravity of the black hole. The matter spirals toward the black hole and gets heated to a few million degrees. Before falling into the black hole, this fiercely hot matter emits huge amounts of X-rays, which we can detect using telescopes in space. From the measurement of these X-rays, astronomers can work out that the object pulling the matter must be a black hole. Since nobody has ever seen a black hole, we can only imagine what they look like. However, this guess is closely based on everything else we have learned about black holes to date.

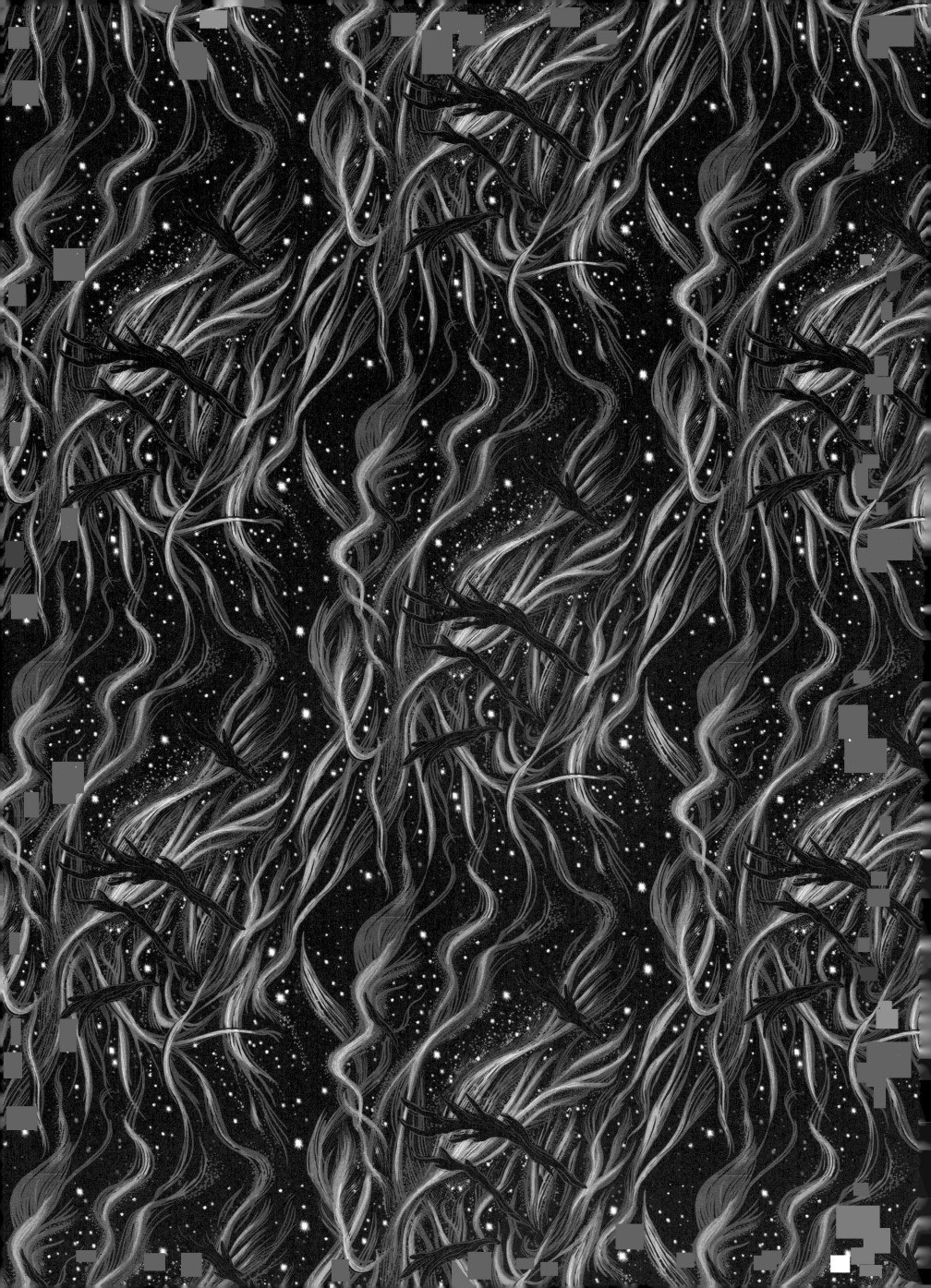

Gallery 6

Galaxies

Galaxy Types
The Milky Way Galaxy
Cosmic Collisions
Galaxy Clusters

Galaxy Types

Scattered across the universe are an estimated two trillion galaxies, each one a vast collection of stars, gas, and dust held together by the force of gravity. They come in many shapes and sizes, but most can be grouped into three main types: spirals, ellipticals, and irregulars.

The most common type of galaxy are spirals, which make up around 75 percent of all galaxies in the universe, including our own Milky Way. They have an almost spherical bulge at their center, packed with ancient red and yellow stars—and in some instances, containing a supermassive black hole. Around the bulge is a flattened disc of gas, dust, and young, bright stars, which can sometimes split into "arms" of matter, spiraling around the bulge and giving the galaxy a pinwheel appearance. Finally, surrounding this is a sphere of ancient stars, a barely visible halo enshrouding the whole galaxy.

The second-most common type are ellipticals, which have an ellipsoidal or egglike shape. These mostly contain old stars and have little gas and dust within them to forge new stars. Ellipticals range in size from dwarfs containing barely a few thousand stars to some of the largest galaxies in the universe. These may be 300 million light-years across and loaded with up to a hundred trillion stars.

Lastly, irregular galaxies, as their name suggests, have no regular shape or structure. They contain lots of gas and dust, which makes them the perfect place for new stars to form, so they are full of luminous, newly born stars.

Astronomers are still trying to understand how galaxies were created in the early history of the universe. One idea is that spiral galaxies formed from vast clouds of gas that were spinning very rapidly, while ellipticals may have formed from clouds that rotated more slowly and made their stars more quickly. Meanwhile, it is widely thought that irregular galaxies arise from collisions between galaxies or as a result of strong gravitational forces distorting them. We still have much to learn about this subject, but thanks to the latest telescopes, we can study galaxies billions of light-years away and catch a glimpse of the time when they first formed.

Key to plate

1: Spiral galaxy

The Messier 83 (M83) is a spiral galaxy in the direction of the constellation Hydra. It spans around 40,000 light-years across, making it almost three times smaller than our galaxy. New generations of stars are being formed in huge clusters toward the inner edges of its spiral arms.

2: Elliptical galaxy

The giant elliptical galaxy called ESO 325-G004 is more than 450 million light-years away in the direction of Centaurus. It has a phenomenal mass around a hundred billion times that of our sun.

3: Irregular galaxy

NGC 4449 is an irregular galaxy nearly 12.5 million light-years away from us. Like most irregular galaxies, it is a site of prolific star formation, including vast numbers of new massive stars that radiate blue and ultraviolet light. The galaxy is around 20,000 light-years across.

The Milky Way Galaxy

Our home galaxy, the Milky Way, is a beautiful spiral galaxy named after its milky white appearance in our skies. Earth lies in a region toward its edge, around 26,000 light-years from the galaxy's center. Unfortunately, this position makes it difficult for scientists on Earth to work out the galaxy's overall shape—especially as a dense cluster of stars, gas, and dust blocks our view. The challenge is a bit like standing in the middle of a forest and trying to determine how it looks from above. However, infrared telescopes can penetrate these dusty clouds, meaning we can build a picture of the galaxy.

Like other spiral galaxies, the shape of the Milky Way galaxy resembles two fried eggs stuck back-to-back: in this analogy, the yolks form the galaxy's central bulge and the whites represent its disc. The flattened disc is around 100,000 light-years across and contains at least two hundred billion stars, all orbiting the galaxy's center. This means that the Milky Way spins like a whirlpool of stars, completing a full rotation once every 220 million years.

As the galaxy rotates, the stars in its farthest outposts orbit its center at remarkable speeds of almost 500,000 miles per hour/800,000 kilometers per hour. But despite their rapid motion, the stars are not flung out of the galaxy as we might expect. Instead, they stay firmly in their positions at the edges of the spiral arms. This remarkable behavior is something all spiral galaxies have in common and has long been a mystery to astronomers. However, scientists have recently discovered how these fast-moving stars remain bound together. The answer is dark matter—vast amounts of unobservable matter that acts like an invisible "glue," binding the galaxy together so it keeps its shape. Not much is known about dark matter yet, as it does not emit any electromagnetic radiation, making it almost impossible to detect. What we do know is that it exerts a gravitational tug on nearby objects. It is this additional tug on distant, high-speed stars that prevents them from escaping our galaxy—and that alerted us to the very existence of dark matter.

Key to plate

1: The Milky Way galaxy (viewed from the side)
a) Bulge: This is thought to have a supermassive black hole four million times the mass of the sun at its center.
b) Disc: The flattened part of a galaxy that extends beyond its central bulge.

c) Halo: An invisible area of dark matter surrounding the disc.

2: The Milky Way galaxy (viewed from above)
a) Bulge
b) Disc

c) Halo
d) Spiral arm: The Milky Way has four major spiral arms, which contain lots of gas, dust, and stellar nurseries. Our solar system is located within a minor spiral arm called the Orion Arm.

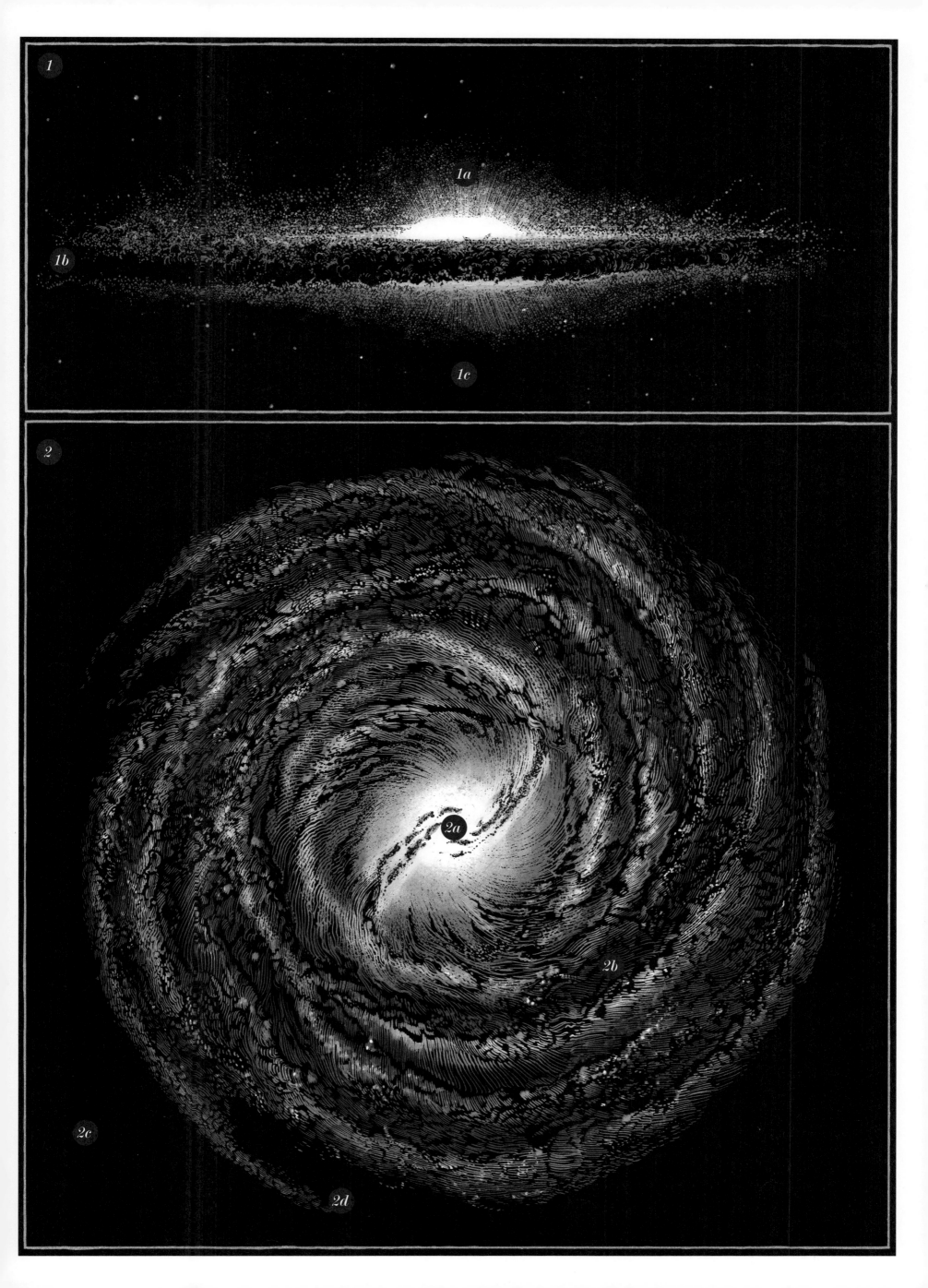

Cosmic Collisions

Most galaxies are not alone in the universe but are relatively close to their neighbors—drawn together by their mutual gravitational force. Sometimes pairs of galaxies get pulled so close to each other that they smash together in spectacular impacts. Astronomers have observed many distant examples of these cosmic collisions, and even our own Milky Way galaxy is on a course to crash billions of years from now.

So what happens when two galaxies collide? Sometimes a small galaxy drifts too close to a giant galaxy, gets stripped of its stars and gas, and eventually gets swallowed up by the larger galaxy. But the collision between two giant galaxies can be far more dramatic, involving enormous structures hundreds of thousands of light-years across and loaded with billions of stars. When these giant galaxies crash, they irreversibly lock together, creating a combined mass equivalent to a hundred trillion suns mixing together over many millions of years.

Since the space between stars is so enormous, there is little chance of two stars hitting when their galaxies collide. It is much more likely that the vast clouds of gas in each galaxy will be squeezed together, triggering millions of stars to burst into life. During this mixing and mingling, great streams of stars can be ripped out of place to form bridges between adjacent galaxies. Alternatively, in some head-on collisions, the supermassive black holes at the centers of both galaxies may merge to make an even more massive black hole.

Astronomers believe most galaxies experience several collisions over the course of their lifetime, and that these impacts are strong enough to drastically and permanently alter their structure and evolution.

Key to plate

1: **"Rose of galaxies"**
These colliding spiral galaxies, together known as Arp 273, have been locked together and distorted to form a stunning roselike shape, sometimes referred to as a "rose of galaxies." The bright central cores of the two galaxies are separated by just over 100,000 light-years. Their coming together has resulted in huge amounts of material being pulled out of each of them. This material forms vast curved tails of gas and dust that stretch away from the outer parts of each galaxy.

Galaxy Clusters

Galaxies are naturally drawn to one another by their powerful gravitational force, so they are usually found in groups known as clusters. These can be small groups of just a dozen or so galaxies, or they can be enormous collections of thousands of galaxies and trillions of stars, spanning millions of light-years across.

We know that bigger objects exert much more gravitational pull than smaller ones. We can even estimate the mass of an object by observing its gravitational pull. However, this presents a bit of a mystery when it comes to galaxy clusters: they must have an incredibly huge mass for their gravity to bind them together—without this, random galaxies would drift away from their neighbors, and clusters would gradually disperse. But when we add together all the detectable mass in a galaxy cluster—including stars, planets, and dust clouds—this total mass is nowhere near big enough to create the kind of gravity we see in action. That means there must be something else adding to the mass of these clusters. And this mysterious substance is known as dark matter. Astronomers think dark matter could be in the form of incredibly tiny particles, each smaller than an atom, which rarely interact with any other matter. Remarkably, almost 85 percent of a typical galaxy cluster's mass may be hidden in its dark matter, providing most of the gravity that holds a cluster together.

Although galaxy clusters are unimaginably huge, they are still not the largest structures in space. This title is held by giant groups of galaxy clusters known as superclusters. Together these span across space like a vast spiderweb, linking the most distant corners of the universe. The origins of superclusters must have been in place soon after the universe started; since then, their structures have been very slowly changing over time. This means that the properties of the largest galaxy superclusters can tell us about the blueprint of the universe in the moments after the big bang (see page 86) and help us to understand how the universe itself evolved.

Key to plate

1: Galaxy cluster

CL0024+17 is a cluster of galaxies about 5 billion light-years away. Astronomers have used detailed observations made with the Hubble Space Telescope to carefully study the spread and shapes of these galaxies.

They have also examined how this cluster bends and distorts the light from even more distant galaxies that lie behind it. From all this information it has been possible to work out a map showing how dark matter is spread around CL0024+17. The predicted

dark matter is shown as the ghostly blue regions surrounding the galaxies. It may be that the dark matter has a ring shape due to the collision between two gigantic galaxy clusters!

The Universe

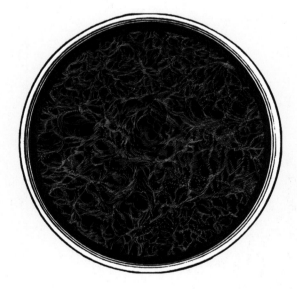

The Universe
The Big Bang
The Runaway Universe
The End of the Universe

The Universe

The universe encompasses everything there is: all of time, energy, and every bit of matter in space, from the tiniest asteroids to the biggest galaxies. Its scientific study is called cosmology, which seeks to answer some of our most profound questions, such as how the universe began, how it will end, and whether there are other universes beyond our own. In order to do this, cosmologists create models for their theories, which make it possible to visualize and predict phenomena we could never possibly observe, including the very earliest days of the universe. These models can then be put to the test by comparing them with observations of galaxies and stars. As our understanding of space evolves, some models are cast aside, while newer ones are constantly emerging.

Over the past two thousand years, there have been three major phases in our understanding of the universe. The first occurred in around 360 BCE, when the Greek philosophers Plato and Aristotle wrote about a geocentric model of the universe. Based on the Greek word *geo*, meaning Earth, this model imagined our planet at the center of everything, with the planets, sun, and stars rotating around it. Standardized by Ptolemy in the second century CE, this theory was widely accepted until the sixteenth century, when the mathematical theories of Copernicus, followed by Isaac Newton's new law of gravity, led to the proposal that the sun was the center of the universe instead. This heliocentric model was named after the Ancient Greek word *helios,* meaning sun. Its vision of the solar system was accurate, but there was still some way to go in understanding our place in the wider universe.

The third revolution in cosmology began in 1915, when Albert Einstein published his general theory of relativity. He outlined that massive objects, such as stars and galaxies, cause space to sag or bend around them — the way a large adult standing on a trampoline will make it sag. Using Einstein's equations, the Belgian physicist Georges Lemaître deduced that the speed of galaxies was proportionate to their distance. He thus concluded that the universe is expanding. Meanwhile, in 1929, Edwin Hubble's observations from the Mount Wilson Observatory in California revealed that galaxies were rapidly moving away from each other. Lemaître used Hubble's discovery as evidence for what we now call the big bang theory — our prevailing model of the universe. This model depicts a universe that began around fourteen billion years ago, has no center, and has been evolving and changing ever since its birth.

Key to plate

1: **The observable universe**
The universe is so huge that parts of it may not even be visible to us yet, as their light signals haven't had time to reach us. We call the part we can see the observable universe. Because light travels at the same speed, this can be thought of as a "bubble" around our planet, growing bigger year after year as more distant light starts to reach us. Here, the observable universe is shown with Earth at its center, surrounded by galaxies and stars. However, we know that the universe in its entirety has no center.

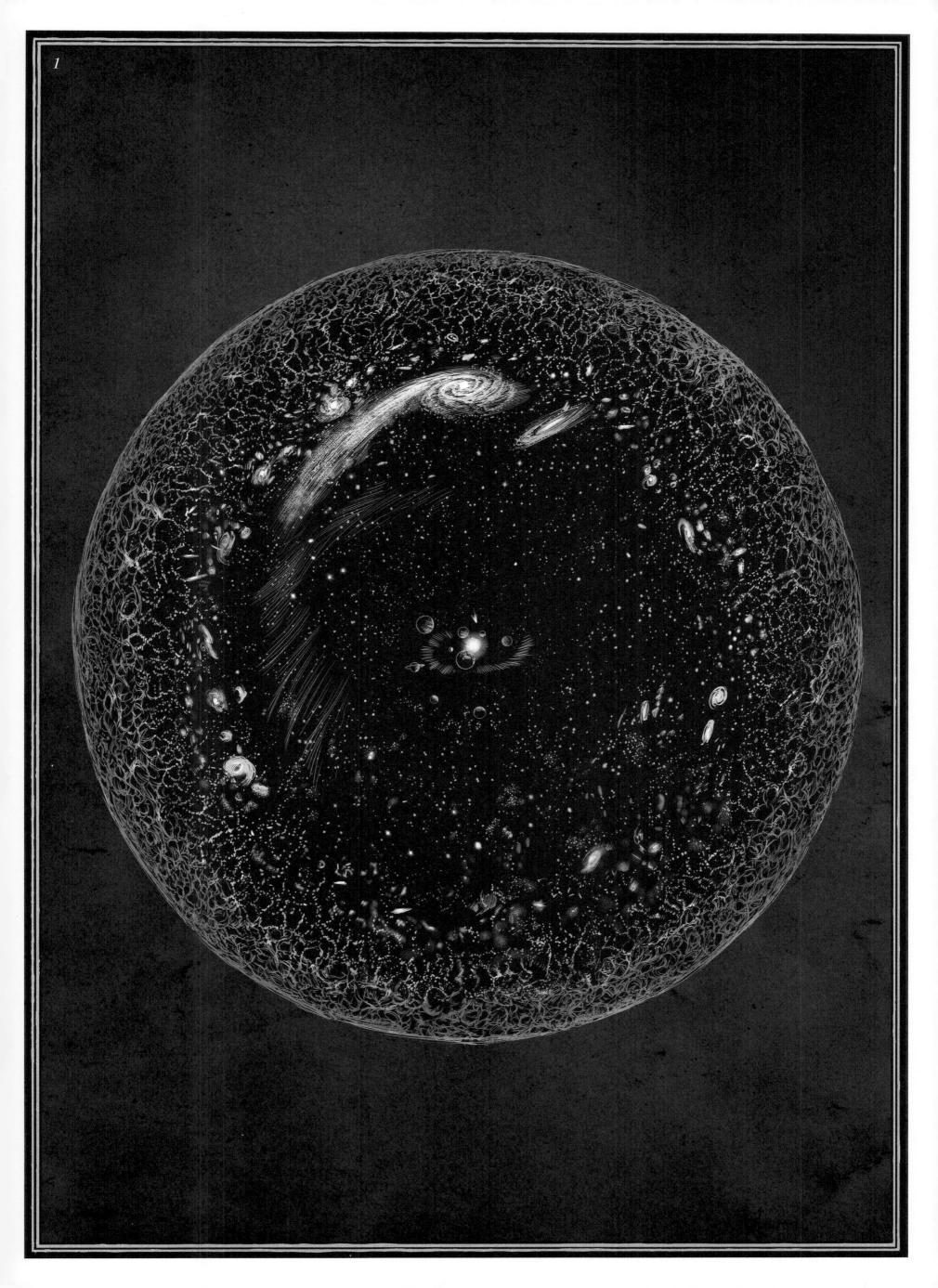

The Big Bang

Most astronomers today believe that the universe emerged from an event called the big bang, which occurred about 13.8 billion years ago. At that time, the whole universe was contained within an incredibly small bubble, thousands of times smaller than the period at the end of this sentence. In an instant, the big bang sparked a rapid inflation of this bubble, flinging energy and matter outward in all directions. Ever since, space has continued stretching outward, carrying matter farther and farther from its initial starting point—the time and place of the big bang.

In the first tiny fraction of a second after the big bang, the universe doubled in size at least ninety times, going from smaller than an atom to the size of a golf ball, with temperatures exceeding 18 trillion°F/10 trillion°C. During the next three minutes, it continued to expand while also cooling to just 1.8 billion°F/1 billion°C. The cooling universe allowed protons and neutrons to combine, forming the lightest elements known to us, such as hydrogen, helium, and a small amount of lithium. (Heavier elements such as carbon, oxygen, and silicon were forged much later inside stars.)

During the next 380,000 years, the universe was still too hot for light to shine from it. Sometimes known as the dark ages in the history of the universe, this state of darkness occurred because light photons were trapped inside the ultra-hot "fog" of the

86

universe. They continually bounced off densely collected particles, such as protons and electrons, but couldn't escape the fog, which meant they were unable to shine.

Finally, when the universe was about 380,000 years old, its temperature dropped to 5,000°F/3,000°C, creating conditions cool enough for electrons to be trapped in orbit around nuclei, forming the first atoms. With more electrons locked into atoms, and fewer floating around, it was finally possible for light to escape. (Today we can detect this as a much cooler form of radiation called cosmic microwave background radiation; it is the oldest light we can see in the universe.) Another three hundred million to five hundred million years after the first light shone, clumps of gas collapsed and squeezed together under gravity, and the very first stars and galaxies were born.

--- ***Key to plate*** ---

1: **The evolving universe**

a) The big bang: The universe begins in a sudden moment of expansion around 13.8 billion years ago.

b) High-energy reactions: The early universe is a "soup" of heat and radiation. This can be detected today as cosmic microwave background radiation.

c) The dark ages of the universe: The first atoms form, but there are still no stars, so the universe is in total darkness.

d) First stars: About two hundred million years after the big bang, the very first stars form.

e) First galaxies: Around one billion years after the big bang, the very first large galaxies form.

f) Accelerating universe: The expansion of the universe starts to rapidly accelerate, owing to a mysterious component of the universe called dark energy.

g) The solar system: About nine billion years after the big bang, our sun forms. The leftover material collects to create the planets of our solar system, including our own planet, Earth.

The Runaway Universe

Since Edwin Hubble's discovery that galaxies are moving away from one another, astronomers have understood that the universe is expanding in the aftermath of the big bang. Now the questions facing astronomers are how rapidly the universe is expanding and whether this expansion is likely to continue forever. If they answer these questions, they may be able to determine how the universe will end.

In the mid-1990s, astronomers set out to accurately measure how fast the universe was expanding. To do this they measured the distances between type la supernovae, which are particularly bright and uniform, making them ideal "markers" in space. The astronomers predicted that their results would show the universe slowing down in its expansion, pulled back by its own gravity as it aged. However, what they actually discovered was that the supernovae were dimmer and farther away than they had anticipated. Instead of slowing down, the universe was expanding at an ever-accelerating rate. It seems we live in a "runaway universe."

This discovery means there has to be a force that's working counter to gravity and pushing the universe apart with increasing speed. Scientists call this mysterious new force dark energy. Nobody is sure what dark energy is, but there must be a lot of it to make the universe accelerate so rapidly. Incredibly, scientists think that ordinary matter, such as planets, stars, and galaxies, only make up 4 percent of matter in the universe. Another 22 percent of matter is dark matter (see pages 76 and 80), such as the subatomic particles that bind galaxy clusters together. Staggeringly, the remaining 74 percent of matter in the universe is thought to be the enigmatic force dark energy.

Key to plate

1: **Runaway universe**
The universe is growing bigger and bigger, and is growing by a larger amount every year. This expansion doesn't have a big effect on the space between planets in our solar system. But long into the future, all the galaxies that we can currently see through our telescopes will have drifted out of view, carried away by the stretching of space. Scientists estimate the acceleration (or expansion rate) of the universe today is about 44 miles per second/70 kilometers per second per 3.26 million light-years.

The End of the Universe

No one is sure what the ultimate fate of the universe will be. Many billions or trillions of years from now, it may be ripped apart, or shrunk down to nothing—or could perhaps remain exactly as it is. Its fate will be determined by the amount of ordinary and dark matter it contains, but will also depend on the behavior of the gravity-opposing force known as dark energy.

Each possible scenario for the end of the universe is based on how the expansion of the universe might behave. They all hinge on the idea that dark energy could potentially change its behavior in the future, though we don't yet know why this would happen. One scenario is that dark energy could someday stop pushing against gravity. If this happens, and if the universe contains sufficient matter, the universe may stop expanding and even start contracting. A hundred billion years from now, all the content of the universe might squeeze down to a single point in a reverse of the big bang. This theory of the collapsing universe is called the big crunch.

Another possibility is that dark energy will become so strong that it eventually overwhelms all forces of nature, including gravity. If this happens, the expansion of the universe will continue to get faster and faster as it is pushed apart without any limit. This end is known as the Big Rip, and would result in galaxies, stars, planets, and all life being torn apart; ultimately, even the atoms that form all matter would be destroyed.

Alternatively, it might turn out that the universe simply continues to expand at a constant rate. If dark energy always exerts the same force as it does today, space will continue to expand, and the distances between galaxies will stretch wider and wider. Eventually, all the galaxies will be pulled too far apart to be seen. In this lonely and dark universe, trillions of years ahead, the temperature would drop to its lowest possible value. In this "Big Chill" ending, the universe would be too cold for any life to survive. All that would remain would be the burned-out corpses of stars, frozen planets, and black holes.

How and if the universe will end are just some of its many mysteries. Even though we are constantly broadening our understanding of the universe, humans have far more to learn than we have already discovered. We have barely scratched the surface of space.

Key to plate

1: **The Big Rip**
The scenario called the Big Rip would see the universe expanding at such a rapid rate that it physically rips itself apart. Whole galaxies, stars, and planets would be torn into countless pieces. And after all the physical objects (bound together by gravity) have been pulled apart, the force of dark energy would then destroy objects such as molecules, atoms, and even subatomic particles, which are held together by other forces. While this destructive picture is just one way in which the universe might end, the good news is that this scenario won't be happening for at least another hundred billion years.

Library

Index
Curators
To Learn More

Index

55 Cancri e (Janssen) 42, 43

Alpha Centauri 58
ammonia 30, 32, 36
Aquarius 58, 59
Aristotle 84
Arp 273 78, 79
Asteroid Belt 38, 41
asteroids 28, 40–41
Atacama Large Millimeter Array
   (ALMA) 12–13
atmospheres
  Earth 14, 24, 48
  Jupiter 30
  Mercury 20
  Neptune 36
  Venus 22
atoms 20, 41, 46, 48, 64, 68, 87
aurora borealis 48

bacterial life 29
Beta Orionis 56
big bang 80, 84, 86–87
Big Chill 90
big crunch 90
Big Dipper 56
Big Rip 90, 91
binary stars 71
black dwarfs 68
black holes 66, 67, 68, 70–71, 74, 78, 90

Callisto 30
Canopus 58
carbon 68, 86
carbon dioxide 22
Carina Nebula 58
Centaurus 58, 59
Ceres 38, 39
Chandra X-ray Observatory 14, 15
chromosphere 46, 47
CL0024+17 80, 81
comets 20, 24, 40–41, 40
Compton Gamma Ray
   Observatory 14

constellations 55, 56
  northern hemisphere 56–57
  southern hemisphere 58–59
Copernicus, Nicolaus 84
coronal loops 46, 47
Coronal Mass Ejection (CME) 48
cosmic microwave background
   radiation 87
cosmology 84
Crab Nebula 68, 69
craters 10, 20, 26, 28, 30, 36
Crux 58

dark energy 87, 88, 90
dark matter 76, 80, 88, 90
Dawn spacecraft 38
Deimos 29
diamond 68
diamond rain 36
dust storms 29
dwarf planets 38, 39
dwarf stars 62, 63, 66, 67, 68

Earth 2, 5, 18, 19, 22, 24–25, 26,
   51, 84, 85
  atmosphere 14, 24, 48
  cosmic address 5
  layers 24
  magnetic field 24, 48, 49
  sun–Earth connection 48–49
earthquakes 24
EBLM J0555-57Ab 62
Einstein, Albert 84
electricity 48
electromagnetic spectrum 8, 9, 14
electrons 46, 68, 87
Eris 38, 39, 51
Eta Carina 58
Europa 30
exoplanets 42
  Earth-like 42
exosphere 24
Extremely Large
   Telescope (E-ELT) 13

galaxies 5, 10, 72–81, 84, 87
  clusters 80–81
  collisions 78
  elliptical 74–75
  irregular 75
  Local Group 5
  "rose of galaxies" 78–79
  spiral 74–75, 76, 78–79
  superclusters 3, 5, 80
  see also Milky Way
Galilean satellites 30
Galileo Galilei 10, 11
Galle, Johann Gottfried 36
gamma rays 8–9, 14
Ganymede 30
gas giants 18, 30–37, 42
"Goldilocks planets" 42
Geminids 55
gravitational waves 71
gravity 18, 26, 28, 38, 41, 42, 46, 51,
   66, 68, 70, 71, 78, 80, 87, 88
Great Dark Spot, Neptune 36, 37
Great Red Spot, Jupiter 30, 31

Haumea 38, 39
heat energy 32, 34, 46, 48, 62
helium 20, 30, 32, 34, 36, 46, 50,
   64, 66, 86
helium balloons 14
Herschel, William 10, 34
Hubble, Edwin 84
Hubble Space Telescope 14, 15, 80
Hydra 58, 59
hydrogen 20, 30, 32, 34, 36, 46, 50,
   51, 64, 66, 86

ice
  methane ice 34
  nitrogen ice 38
  water ice 20, 29, 30, 33, 36
ice giants 34
infrared radiation 8, 9, 13, 14
International Astronomical
   Union (IAU) 56

International Space Station 24
Io 30
ions 46
iron 20, 24
iron oxide 28

James Webb Space Telescope 14, 15
Jewel Box cluster 58
Jupiter 10, 18, 19, 30–31, 42, 54

Keck Observatory 12–13
Kuiper Belt 38, 40

Laniakea Supercluster 2, 5
Large and Small Magellanic Clouds 58
Laser Interferometer Gravitational-
   Wave Observatory (LIGO) 71
lava flows 20, 23, 42
lava plains 23, 26
Le Verrier, Urbain 36
Lemaître, Georges 84
Leonids 55
Lick, James 10
life-forms 24, 29, 33, 42, 48
light 8, 10
  speed of light 5
  visible light 8–9, 12, 13, 14
light-years 5
lithium 86
Local Group 3, 5
Lyrids 55

Maat Mons, Venus 23
Magellan spacecraft 23
magnetic fields 20, 24, 30, 48, 49, 68
magnetosphere 48
Makemake 38–39
Mars 18, 19, 28–29, 54
mass 18, 28, 32, 46, 66, 68
Mercury 18, 19, 20–21, 51, 54
mesosphere 24
MESSENGER probe 20
Messier 83 (M83) 74, 75
meteorites 41

meteoroids 20, 24, 41

meteors 24, 41

  meteor showers 55

methane 33, 36, 42

methane ice 34, 36

microwaves 8–9

Milky Way 3, 5, 42, 54–55, 58, 64, 74, 76–77, 78

Miranda 34, 35

moon 26–27, 48

  craters 10, 26

  landings 26

  phases 26, 27

moons 18, 29, 30, 31, 33, 34, 35, 36

NASA 14, 38

nebulae 64, 66, 67, 68, 69

Neptune 5, 18, 19, 36, 37

neutron stars 66, 68

neutrons 68, 86

New Horizons spacecraft 38

Newton, Isaac 84

NGC 4449 75

nickel 20, 24

night sky 52–59

nitrogen 33, 36

nitrogen ice 38

NML Cygni 62–63

nuclear fusion 46, 50, 64, 66

observatories 12–13

  space observatories 14–15

Olympus Mons, Mars 28, 29

Oort Cloud 40, 41

Orion 56

Orion Nebula 64, 65, 76

Orionids 55

oxygen 24, 42, 86

ozone 24, 42

Phobos 29

photons 86

photosphere 46, 47

planetary rings 30, 32–33, 34, 35

planets

  dwarf planets 38, 39

  exoplanets 42

  gas planets 18, 30–37, 42

  "Goldilocks planets" 42

  planetesimals 64

  terrestrial rocky planets 18, 20–25, 28–29

  see also individual index entries

plasma 46, 48

Plato 84

Plough 56

Pluto 18, 38–39

Polaris (polestar) 56

protons 86, 87

protostars 64, 66, 67

Ptolemy 84

radial velocity method 42

radiation 8–9, 14, 24, 48, 62, 64, 87

radio waves 8–9, 13

rainbows 8

red giants 50–51, 66, 67

relativity theory 84

rocky planets 18, 20–25, 28–29

sand dunes 23

satellites 14

Saturn 10, 18, 19, 32–33, 54–55

shooting stars see meteors

silicon 86

Sirius 58

solar corona 46, 47, 48, 49

solar cycle 48

solar eclipse 48, 49

solar flares 46, 47, 48

solar system 2, 5, 17–43, 87

  comets and asteroids 20, 24, 28, 40–41

  formation 18

  moon 20, 26, 27, 48

  moons 18, 29, 30, 31, 33, 34, 35, 36

space debris 24, 41

solar wind 20, 40, 48

Southern Cross 58

space debris 24, 41

spacecraft 20, 22, 23, 29, 30, 38

spectroscopes 10

Spitzer Space Telescope 14, 15

star charts 56, 57, 58, 59

stars 5, 10, 42, 54–55, 60–71, 74, 78, 84

  binaries 71

  birth of 8, 64, 65, 87

  brightness 42, 54

  collision 8

  color 54–55

  constellations 55, 56–59, 57, 59

  death of 50–51, 66, 68, 69

  dwarf stars 62, 63, 66, 67, 68

  giants and supergiants 50–51, 62–63, 66, 67

  life cycle 63, 66, 67

  mass 66, 68

  neutron stars 66, 68

  orbits 55

  protostars 64, 66, 67

  star types 62–63

  temperatures 62–63, 64

storms 29, 30, 32, 34, 36

stratosphere 24

sulfur 30

sulfuric acid 22

sun 5, 18, 19, 20, 34, 42, 44–51, 47, 62, 84

  coronal loops 46, 47

  coronal mass ejection (CME) 48

  death of 50–51

  formation 18

  gravity 18, 46, 51

  layers 46, 47

  solar corona 46, 47, 48, 49

  solar cycle 48

  solar flares 46, 47, 48

  sunspots 46, 47, 48

  sun–Earth connection 48, 49

sunspots 46, 47, 48

supernovae 58, 66, 67, 68, 69, 70, 88

tectonic plates 24

telescopes 10–15, 11

  infrared 64, 76

  reflecting 10, 11

  refracting 10, 11, 12

  space telescopes 14, 15

thermosphere 24

thunderstorms 22

Titan 33

Triton 36

troposphere 24

ultraviolet radiation 8, 9, 14

universe 5, 13, 82–91

  big bang 80, 84, 86–87

  dark ages 86, 87

  end of 90

  expansion of 84, 86, 87, 88, 89, 90

  geocentric model 84

  heliocentric model 84

  observable universe 84, 85

Uranus 18, 19, 34, 35

Ursa Major 56

Venus 18, 19, 22–23, 51, 54

Venus Express spacecraft 23

Very Large Telescope (VLT) 12–13

Virgo Supercluster 3, 5

volcanoes 23, 24, 26, 30

water

  ice 20, 29, 30, 33, 36

  liquid 24, 29, 42, 48, 51

  vapor 24

wavelengths 8

white dwarfs 63, 66, 67, 68

winds 28, 30, 32, 36

  see also solar wind

X-rays 8, 9, 14, 71

Curators

Chris Wormell is a self-taught engraver and celebrated printmaker.
He creates his timeless illustrations using wood engraving and linocut, as well as
digital engraving. He has written and illustrated many children's books and most
recently gained recognition for his cover illustrations for the award-winning,
best-selling *H Is for Hawk* by Helen Macdonald and for Philip Pullman's
The Book of Dust, Volume One: La Belle Sauvage.

Raman Prinja is professor of astrophysics at University College London, where he
specializes in massive stars, star formation, and the evolution of galaxies. He is a winner
of multiple UCL faculty and department teaching awards. He is eager to bring the
subject of astronomy to a wider audience and has written several successful
books on the subject, including *Night Sky Watcher*, which was short-listed
for the Royal Society Young People's Book Prize in 2015.

To Learn More

The European Space Agency (ESA)
Europe's gateway to space, featuring
the latest news on space flight,
telecommunications, and exploration.
www.esa.int

Galaxy Zoo
Try your hand at classifying galaxies,
and join an amazing citizen science
project.
www.galaxyzoo.org

Google Sky
This provides an engaging way to
explore the universe and see what's
happening in the sky tonight. You can
also look at the surface of the moon
or Mars using the Google Maps tool.
www.google.com/sky

Hubblesite
Discover all the latest from the
Hubble space probe on this website of
stunning photographs, articles, and live
telescope views.
http://hubblesite.org

In-The-Sky.org
The ideal tool for stargazing,
showing exactly what's in the night
sky wherever you are in the world.
https://in-the-sky.org

**National Aeronautics and Space
Administration (NASA)**
Providing cutting-edge news, videos,
and images from the world's largest
space agency. NASA TV also provides
live coverage of launches, spacewalks,
and other events.
www.nasa.gov

NASA Astronomy Picture of the Day
An amazing collection of the latest
images from space.
https://apod.nasa.gov

Science Museum Collections Online
Explore more than 250,000 objects
and archives from the museum's
collection.
https://collection.sciencemuseum
.org.uk

**Smithsonian National Air
and Space Museum**
Find out more about space
exploration.
https://airandspace.si.edu

Space
Access all the latest astronomy news
and articles on space exploration.
www.space.com

SpaceNews
News of astronomy, space exploration,
and commercial spaceflight.
www.spacenews.com

The Sun Today
Look at what's happening on the sun
every day, and learn about the space
weather around us.
www.thesuntoday.org

The Universe Today
Keep up-to-date with all the latest
space-related news.
www.universetoday.com